The Financial
Revolution
1660–1760

Henry Roseveare

LONGMAN
London and New York

Longman Group UK Limited,
Longman House, Burnt Mill, Harlow,
Essex CM20 2JE, England
and Associated Companies throughout the world.

Published in the United States of America
by Longman Inc., New York.

© Longman Group UK Limited 1991

All rights reserved; no part of this publication may be reproduced, stored in
a retrieval system, or transmitted in any form or by any means, electronic,
mechanical, photocopying, recording, or otherwise, without either the prior
written permission of the Publishers or a licence permitting restricted
copying issued by the Copyright Licence Agency Ltd., 33–34 Alfred Place,
London WC1E 7DP.

First published 1991

Set in 10/11 point Baskerville (Linotron)
Produced by Longman Malaysia Sdn Berhad
Printed in Malaysia
by Vinlin Press Sdn. Bhd., Sri Petaling, Kuala Lumpur

ISBN 0 582 35449 8

British Library Cataloguing in Publication Data
Roseveare, Henry
   The financial revolution.
   1. England, history. Finance
   I. Title
   332.0942

   ISBN 0-582-35449-8

Library of Congress Cataloging-in-Publication Data
Roseveare, Henry.
      The financial revolution, 1660–1760 / Henry Roseveare.
         p.   cm. – (Seminar studies in history)
      Includes bibliographical references and index.
      ISBN 0-582-35449-8
      1. Debts, Public – Great Britain – History.
      2. Finance, Public – Great Britain – History.   I. Title.
      II. Series.
      HJ8623.R67   1991   90-27758
      336.42 – dc20   CIP

Contents

Contents

Seminar Studies in History
Founding Editor: Patrick Richardson

Introduction

The Seminar Studies series was conceived by Patrick Richardson, whose experience of teaching history persuaded him of the need for something more substantial than a textbook chapter but less formidable than the specialised full-length academic work. He was also convinced that such studies, although limited in length, should provide an up-to-date and authoritative introduction to the topic under discussion as well as a selection of relevant documents and a comprehensive bibliography.

Patrick Richardson died in 1979, but by that time the Seminar Studies series was firmly established, and it continues to fulfil the role he intended for it. This book, like others in the series, is therefore a living tribute to a gifted and original teacher.

Note on the System of References:
A bold number in round brackets (**5**) in the text refers the reader to the corresponding entry in the Bibliography section at the end of the book. A bold number in square brackets, preceded by 'doc.' **[doc. 6]** refers the reader to the corresponding item in the section of Documents, which follows the main text. Items followed by an asterisk * are explained in the Glossary.

ROGER LOCKYER
General Editor

v

Preface and Acknowledgements

The concept of a 'Financial Revolution' analogous to the 'Industrial Revolution', both in its duration and significance for English history, was firmly established by Peter Dickson in 1967. His seminal book of well over 500 pages (**72**) was a masterly study reflecting research on the financial system of eighteenth-century England which has not been, and probably need not be, superseded. Dickson's painstaking analysis of the records of the Bank of England, the Treasury, Exchequer and other key institutions and companies such as the East India Company, established a solid framework of facts and probabilities about public borrowing, banking, investment and the rate of interest upon which subsequent financial historians can safely rely. I have drawn heavily upon it in what follows.

However, when reviewing the book on its first appearance, I expressed some reservation about its terminal dates which I feared 'compounded the fallacy of discontinuous development in English financial history' (**172**). In less pompous words, I was not particularly happy with 1688 as the abrupt commencement of Dickson's account and would have preferred a fuller assessment of its background. This short study is, in part, a belated attempt to make good that deficiency and also an effort to review as concisely as possible the several facets of a very complex process which was never purely 'financial' or wholly economic in its significance, for it affected England's history in several ways and at several points – in its politics, its constitution, its society and its international standing.

In trying to draw upon that large canvas I have incurred many other debts, some of which are of considerable antiquity. I am particularly grateful to Professor Donald Coleman, Dr Peter Earle, Professor Henry Horwitz, Dr Dwyryd Jones, Mr John Keyworth, Professor Frank Melton, Dr Glenn Nichols, Professor Jacob Price, Professor Clayton Roberts, Ted Rowlands MP, and Professor Charles Wilson, not merely for reasons which will be largely apparent from my bibliography but for information, ideas and salutary criticisms conveyed over the years. None of them, however, carries the least responsibility for the shortcomings of this book.

Its completion, on the other hand, owes much to the courtesy and efficiency of several libraries and archives and, above all, to the Goldsmiths' Library of the University of London and to the British Library of Political and Economic Science, London School of Economics. But there is also a debt nearer home, to my colleagues and students in the Department of History at King's College, London, for their patience and encouragement, and it is to them that I gratefully dedicate this book.

Cover Hogarth's engraving: *The South Sea Scheme*. The Mansell Collection.

William Hogarth's engraving *The South Sea Scheme* is full of satirical allusions to the disastrous investment mania of 1720 known as 'the Bubble'. From the left, a mountebank devil dismembers 'Fortune' ignored by clergy gambling with dice; deluded investors from all walks of society ride the whirligig of folly (*centre*) while 'Honesty' is broken on the wheel, 'Honour' flogged and 'Trade' expires (*right foreground*). The monumental pillar (*right*), mimicking that erected to mark the Great Fire of 1666, commemorates metaphorically the comparable financial devastation of the City of London in 1720.

We are indebted to Oxford University Press for permission to reproduce an extract from *The Parliamentary Diary of Narcissus Luttrell 1691–93* edited by Henry Horwitz (1972).

Introduction

The Wars now adays seem rather to be waged with Gold than with Iron, and unless we Pay well, we shall never be able to Punish well.

Observations Upon the Bank of England [1695]

The sinews of war

Military prowess is not the only, and certainly not the most desirable, measure of a nation's financial vitality, but it remains a significant one, and there is perhaps no more telling justification for the chronological boundaries chosen for this book than England's contrasting fortunes in the 1660s and the 1760s.

In the middle of the 1660s England fought a second round in its maritime conflict with the Dutch. The war which began in 1665 was not without its naval triumphs, but they were eclipsed by the humiliations of 1667 when the resilient enemy's fleet, unaided by their French ally, sailed virtually unopposed into the anchorages at Chatham, burning several vessels and towing off the flagship, *The Royal Charles*, a trophy of which still adorns the Rijksmuseum in Amsterdam today. In the ensuing peace settlement England got off fairly lightly, yielding up territorial claims in North and South America, the East and West Indies and on the west coast of Africa, but retaining such unconsidered trifles as New Jersey and New Amsterdam (better known to history as New York). Even these could not efface the reality of a resounding defeat which derived in large part from the mismanagement and financial inadequacies of English government.

Less than a century later the picture is rather different. In 1763 Great Britain emerged triumphant from the Seven Years War, having successfully fought France, and intermittently Spain, across four continents and the oceans of the world. This war was not without its reverses, but a string of victories after 1759 left Britain at the zenith of its first Empire, securely possessed of much of North America and India and more firmly entrenched in West Africa and the

1

East and West Indies. The subsequent peace treaty was unpopular, not for its enforced losses but for its magnanimous concessions, handing back, as it did, so many rich spoils – Havana, Guadeloupe, Martinique, St Lucia, Minorca, and so on – to their French and Spanish claimants.

What accounted for this reversal of military fortunes? Were the Britons of the 1760s braver than the English of the 1660s? Were their ships and arms superior? Were they better led? There are many more such questions to pose and even more answers to ponder, but from all the conceivable measures of power – manpower, firepower, will-power – one element stands out as significantly greater in the 1760s, and that is the financial power of British government. England in the 1660s, with a population of *c.* 5.5 million, had staggered under a tax burden of barely £2.5 million. Its government was financially exhausted and scarcely able to defend its commercial heart. In 1763, on the other hand, with a population of about 8 million, Great Britain was supporting a National Debt of £130 million and public expenditure of up to £20 million p.a. She had financed her own campaigns with comparative ease and had sustained her allies to the tune of some £9.3 million. It was an achievement which is not explicable purely in terms of economic growth, for it has been convincingly argued that the resources of mid-eighteenth-century Britain had not grown in proportion to the demands being placed upon them (**152**). On the contrary, comparative studies have shown that England's economy was the most heavily burdened in western Europe and sustained much higher per capita taxation than the French (**136**). The explanation therefore appears to lie elsewhere, in a complex of social, political, administrative and constitutional developments which transformed the willingness, rather than the ability, of English people to pay high taxes, lend large sums and, above all, repose great trust in the financial integrity of their parliamentary government. It is this striking achievement which we have learned to call the 'Financial Revolution'.

Revolution or evolution?

Regrettably, 'revolution' is one of the most overworked terms in the historian's vocabulary, glibly invoked to give some spurious drama and significance to developments which could be more fairly described as 'evolution'. Indeed, sooner or later many of our cherished 'revolutions' – educational, administrative, intellectual and even industrial (**83**) – suffer this re-definition and are shown to have antecedents or discontinuities which spoil their symmetry and dissolve their cohesion. We are often left with duller, but perhaps more faithful, pictures of the nature of change as a hesitant progression, sometimes long in gestation, unplanned or improvised and possibly even unperceived by its participants, with unclear boundaries to mark its beginning or its end.

Such may, or may not, be the real nature of the 'Financial Revolution'. My reflections on that can properly be deferred. But certainly this book does not set out from the unthinking assumption that there was such a thing as a 'revolution', and in choosing to begin in the 1660s I have deliberately set out to detach the origins of these financial developments from the company of another well-attested but controversial revolution – the 'Glorious' one of 1688. Too often it has been assumed that the developments which transformed England's financial potency in the eighteenth century took their departure from the expulsion of James II and the arrival of Dutch William, with Dutch banking, Dutch stock-jobbing, Dutch taxes and all the other paraphernalia of 'Dutch finance' in his baggage. That is, at best, a half-truth, and after a reign of 300 years as the whole truth it is more than time that it made way for the other half – that seventeenth-century England had laboured long to produce a radical transformation of its financial system which would make it the superior of any of its foreign models, and that some of the most important stages in that effort took place in the reign of Charles II.

The parameters of credit

But before plunging into that argument it would be wise to reconsider the breadth and diversity of the issues involved.

For most laymen the financial revolution means little more than the foundation of the Bank of England, the beginnings of a National Debt and the emergence of a stock market – a rather dull story of institutional development brightened only by the melodrama of the 'South Sea Bubble'. But a moment's reflection soon suggests that it must involve much more. For behind these far-reaching innovations lay the security guaranteed by a sovereign parliament within which the power of the purse was unchallengeably rooted in the House of Commons. From this fundamental constitutional basis alone could arise the unprecedented structure of 'national', as opposed to royal, debts. Rising from under £2 million in the 1680s to over £130 million in the 1760s, it was a phenomenon which alternately thrilled and dismayed its observers, and which bred some profound social and political consequences. For its burden and its rewards seemed not to be equally shared, and an influential but over-taxed 'landed interest' glared with increasing bitterness at the profits enjoyed at public expense by a powerful 'monied interest'. Their antagonism is a major theme in the social history of eighteenth-century England and a formative influence on its party-politics (**71, 102, 184**). Yet, despite its evident imperfections, the fiscal system of eighteenth-century England is remarkable for its comparative efficiency and for its successful conciliation – particularly in the case of the Land Tax (**40, 44, 196**) – of those who carried its burden. For, accompanying these constitutional, political and fiscal 'revolutions', there was something of an administrative revolution – or, at least, a striking growth in the power and effectiveness of the state which manifested itself not merely in war but in the subtler tasks of peace (**43**). This enhanced effectiveness was rooted in several improvements – in the greater professionalism of public servants (**103**), in a better command of information and in a superior differentiation of functions which brought into being new and specialised departments, such as the Board of Trade. The enhanced power is also reflected in civilian administration and particularly in the emergence of the Treasury as the dominant organ of government, undisputed guardian of the public purse, master of many subordinate departments and the natural seat of that controversial novelty, the 'premier minister' (**39, 173**).

Yet this is to speak only of the 'public sector'. Beyond these still comparatively modest structures of English government lay an economy and society in which the growth of savings and investment, banking and borrowing followed paths which were influenced, but not entirely dominated, by the requirements of the state. The accumulations of wealth generated by trade, industry and agriculture, which were crucial to the borrowings of government, therefore had to be coaxed and courted, serviced and restored if they were to become part of a virtuous cycle of credit, rather than a vicious circle of debt. Credit, in the sense of trust, is in fact the elusive but fundamental key to the whole story. It was credit which kept the country afloat during the costly wars of the century and drew to England the funds of international investors; credit founded upon a secure constitution and a stable political system; credit assured by efficient administration and equitable taxation; credit guaranteed by a buoyant economy and a sophisticated system of banking and investment. These are some of the diverse components of the

'Financial Revolution' and they provide themes for a much bigger book than this one, but in what follows I have tried to provide a summary and a guide to complexities which, for all their apparent aridity, were to prove vital to Britain's emergence as a 'Great Power'.

Part One: 1660–1685

1   The Legacies of the Interregnum

There has always been a temptation, to which few historians now submit, to restart English history in 1660 and let events unfold without a backward glance. But one of the most interesting features of the Restoration Settlement which followed Charles II's return is its assimilation of many of the most valuable financial legacies of the preceding decades, two of which were of profound and long-term significance.

Revenue

The first of these was the explicit recognition that the normal yearly costs of government could be accurately assessed and provided for by the nation's representatives in Parliament. Such calculations had rarely been attempted before the seventeenth century and were hardly possible in the early years of the Civil War, but by 1653 it was reckoned that, setting military expenditure aside, £200,000 p.a. should suffice for the ordinary costs of day-to-day government, and this sum was specifically written in to the 'Instrument of Government', the constitution under which Cromwell was to govern the British Isles. In 1657 his Parliament was prepared to be even more specific and declared

> our willingness to settle forthwith a yearly revenue of £1,300,000, whereof £1,000,000 for the navy and army, and £300,000 for the support of the Government . . . and to grant such other temporary supplies, according as the Commons assembled in Parliament shall from time to time adjudge the necessities of these nations to require. (**11**, p. 453).

Such a pledge was only possible in a carefully groomed assembly, but, unspontaneous though it was, it represents a notable advance on anything that had been achieved in preceding generations. No earlier English government had been able to elicit such a commitment. Conventionally, kings and queens had been required to 'live of[f] their own', meeting the undifferentiated costs of ruling from

6

the medley of hereditary resources they were supposed to command. These ranged from the revenues of the once-vast crown estates to meagre fees from the custody of idiots, supplemented by the normal life grant of Customs* duties and occasional 'extraordinary' taxes voted by Parliament. The last major effort to reconsider this anachronistic mismatch between the growing requirements of government and the shrinking resources of the crown had been the abortive 'Great Contract'* scheme of 1610 which had foundered upon the House of Commons' reluctance to underwrite a government which they fundamentally distrusted. This traditional English reluctance to face up to financial realities makes it all the more remarkable that Charles II's first Parliament should have carried over to the restored monarchy the principle laid down by the republic:

> That the present King's Majesty's Revenue shall be made up [to] Twelve hundred thousand Pounds a Year. (**15**, vol. 8, p. 150)

Taxation

However, it was one thing to assert the principle; quite another to pay for it. But here too the Civil War was crucial in habituating Englishmen to unprecedented levels of taxation, prised from them by novel means. Fiscal innovation was, in fact, long overdue. The traditional forms of direct taxation by Parliament – the 'Fifteenths and Tenths' devised in the fourteenth century and the 'Subsidy' introduced in the early sixteenth century – were hopelessly out of touch with the actual levels and distribution of English wealth (**181**, **192**). In 1645 they were, of necessity, superseded by a new and carefully calculated levy – the monthly 'Assessment' upon individual counties which in turn re-distributed the burden among their principal men of property. Although goods, chattels, stock and official salaries were supposed to be rated, this was, in effect, a tax on land, and a highly contentious one, which was only reluctantly revived by Charles II's Parliament in 1664 (**24**, pp. 670–5). It was to remain a major form of direct taxation until superseded by the more ambitious 'Land Tax' of 1692 (**40**).

Yet the most resented of the Civil War's fiscal innovations were the Excise* duties introduced in 1643. Falling initially upon a wide range of commodities such as meat, butter, salt, soap, spices and textiles, the Excise tended to draw the bulk of its yield from beers, ale, ciders and spirits, which was quite enough to offend a hard-drinking nation (**43**). But, worse still, it was an alien tax (borrowed from the Dutch) which was alarmingly effective and devoted largely to the upkeep of an unpopular standing army. It required another painful adjustment for MPs to admit that its buoyant yield and broad distribution made it difficult to discard, even in conditions of peace and normality. Thus the Restoration Parliament struggled only briefly with its natural distaste for the Excise before perpetuating it as a permanent element in the crown's revenues (**50**). Expected to produce over £400,000 p.a., the Excise soon rivalled the reformed Customs duties in yield, and with its skilled, up-to-date administration it outshone its rival as an efficient agency of strong modern government (**43**).

Borrowing

The restored monarchy was thus much the healthier for its fiscal legacies from the Civil War, but even new and effective taxation could not solve the most persistent financial problem of any government. For at all times and in all systems there remains an awkward hiatus between needing and receiving money which has to be bridged by borrowing – and for governments, as for individuals, the process of borrowing could be a delicate, painful and disappointing one which tested to the limit the tact, ingenuity and – above all – the credit of the borrower. It also required the existence of a lender.

In this respect early English governments had rarely been at a total loss. Large-scale borrowing had usually been possible – from Jews in the twelfth century, Italians in the fourteenth century, Netherlanders in the sixteenth century and from wealthy Londoners and merchants at almost any time – but it had never been easy or particularly cheap. Sovereign princes always could, and sometimes did, repudiate their debts or enforce unfair terms of repayment, and their betrayals of trust tended to rebound on their successors. Thus the comparatively thrifty Charles I was made to pay a high price for the unreliability of his father, and during his 'personal rule' in the 1630s the domestic sources of government loans were confined to a steadily narrowing circle of companies, contractors and courtiers with vested interests in royal favour (**34**). Motives for lending to a sovereign prince were never pure, and hanging over many of the crown's solicitations for loans was a subtle threat of coercion – or, at least, a clear hint of the subject's obligation to lend money when asked (**90**). There was often little to choose between the notorious 'Forced Loans' of this reign and the seemingly spontaneous loans and 'benevolences' which accompanied them. The rate of interest consequently played little part as an inducement to lend. Fixed at a ceiling of 10% by the usury* legislation of 1571, the legal maximum was reduced to 8% in 1624, and while this was a fair reflection of the maximum price for private transactions it was an unreal index of the government's credit (**34**). Only the crown's privilege and power enabled it to enforce this inadequate rate for its extensive borrowing and tardy repayments.

The private sector

Contemporary opinion was not indifferent to these serious shortcomings in 'public sector' borrowing, but it was also becoming increasingly preoccupied with the limitations of the private sector. The 1620s in particular, with their experience of an acute commercial crisis, witnessed a vigorous debate on economic reform which addressed itself not merely to trade and industry but also to interest rates and exchange rates, currency and banking (**24, 186**). The solution of problems relating to the provision of credit was coming to be seen as an essential step in economic regeneration.

Yet credit – which was universally needed – was almost universally given. The poor sought and got credit at the pawnshops; the well-to-do got credit on bonds and mortgages; the merchant and tradesman habitually bought and sold upon credit. But at every level there were constraints, obstacles and deficiencies of supply. For the poor, the usury laws provided little real protection against extortion; for the well-to-do the legal penalties consequent upon default were very severe, and for merchants and tradesmen the supply of credit was always too tardy, too costly and too small.

There could be no single solution for all these problems, but out of the burgeoning literature of the 1620s which marks the birth of English economic theory, certain common themes for financial reform emerged (**32, 199**). One was the case for lowering interest rates by law – an idea which started a long debate that runs through John Locke to Maynard Keynes. Another was a plea for the foundation of banks. Both arguments derived much of their force from successful foreign examples, for with their experience of Italy, Germany, Spain and the Netherlands, writers such as Gerard de Malynes, Thomas Mun, and Edward Misselden were able to carry conviction by adducing the flourishing banks and moderate interest rates of the most successful economies in western Europe [**doc. 1**].

Banks and bankers

Bankers – men who lent their own and other people's money, who took and gave interest on loans and deposits, who dealt in merchants' bills of exchange* and guarded the savings of ordinary men and women – were no novelty in early modern Europe. The age of the great Renaissance bankers – the Fuggers, Welsers and Medici – had only just passed, and England itself could boast of several wealthy financiers who performed some of the functions we would recognise today as 'banking'. They were not specialists. They might be merchants, like Sir Paul Pindar, or lawyers, like Hugh Audley, or court jewellers like Sir Peter Vanlore, but several of the essential financial services which we require today were performed in some way by someone. Thus, one could lend, or borrow, upon mortgage through the agency of scriveners – professional lawyers skilled in drafting conveyances, who extended their functions to the introduction of clients and the investment of their funds (**58, 139**). One could transfer money across the country, either in cash through the network of drovers and carriers or more safely in paper, by an inland bill of exchange bought through a broker. And if one had a deposit account with a merchant or tradesman 'banker' one might draw upon it a written note which was a cheque in all but name. Paper documents, signed and sometimes sealed, were extensively used to record an obligation to pay up at a future date, and long before that date arrived the paper could be sold and assigned by an endorsement to a succession of owners, thus becoming in effect a cumbersome kind of paper currency. It has been ingeniously calculated that, by the beginning of the seventeenth century, the ratio of such paper credit to circulating coin was at least 12:1 (**126**, p. 99).

Why then was it necessary for Gerard de Malynes to lecture his adopted countrymen on the nature of banks and the shortcomings of England's commercial practices? Clearly, in both areas she still lagged behind the best Continental examples, and one can deduce that he and others had been particularly impressed by the recent foundations of civic and state banks abroad – at Genoa in 1586, Venice in 1587, Milan in 1593, Amsterdam in 1609 and 1614, and Hamburg in 1619. Malynes' definition of a bank in 1622 was therefore rather different from anything known in England [**doc. 1**] but answered a need which thinking men were beginning to discern. Thus, over the next three decades the proposal for a national bank, taking deposits, issuing loans and underwriting the private, public and international credit of the country resurfaced in tract after tract.

By 1652, one of the most eloquent advocates for reform (Henry Robinson, 1605–73?) could hail such a bank as 'the Elixir or Philosopher's Stone' which could solve nearly all the country's economic problems (**24**, p. 651).

The Civil War

Not surprisingly, such an ambitious solution remained beyond the reach of a nation embroiled in civil war. Just before its very outset, in 1640, Charles I had struck an ill-considered blow against any such development by appropriating the commercial bullion reserves held in the Tower of London. He thus ensured that for generations to come men would wonder whether any modern bank was safe under a king. Even under the Parliamentary republic established in 1649 the state's credit was little better, and in the calmer waters of 1657 it could be said that 'the Public Faith [i.e. credit] of the nation is now become a public despair' (**24**, p. 662).

The Parliamentarian cause, strongly entrenched in London, had indeed been favourably placed to call upon superior financial resources, able to raise loans from the corporation of the City, the great livery companies and from the syndicates of businessmen who managed the collection of the Excise* and the Customs*. The state appealed repeatedly to the loyalty and self-sacrifice of its supporters, but in a context of deficient tax yields and unpredictable expenditure, it could offer little sound security to its creditors, and the financial history of the Cromwellian Protectorate is littered with delayed and dishonoured public debts (**33**, **88**).

Yet even in these troubled waters there were rich pickings for private speculators, for despite heavy taxes and the spoliations of war there was evidently money about, seeking and finding profitable reinvestments. The huge land sales of confiscated crown, church and Royalist estates created a speculative market in which the soldiers, paid in paper 'debentures', were obliged to sell at a discount* (**87**). Some proportion of mercantile capital, immobilised by a succession of foreign wars, was probably available for just such opportunities, and it is perhaps indicative of the supply of money that the rate of interest was again reduced in 1651 from 8 to 6%.

The beginnings of English banking?

In channelling these liquid resources towards interest-bearing investments the scriveners* played their customary role and Robert

Abbott, one of the most successful, is known to have handled clients' deposits totalling £1,137,646 in the course of the three years following 1652 (**139**). Much of this may have been loaned on mortgages* to his Royalist clientele, for the defeated supporters of Charles I were often successful in repurchasing their estates before the Restoration in 1660. Some, indeed, may have been successful in holding on to their more liquid assets, for it is a long-established belief that the origin of English banking lies in the guardianship of Royalists' wealth by the goldsmiths of Lombard Street [**doc. 5**].

This celebrated account of the origins of 'goldsmith-banking' has been rightly questioned as rather too neat and far too dramatic. The truth is probably less exciting: that the goldsmiths had been quietly developing their financial activities for some time, and that the 'safe-deposit' function was only the most basic of the services they performed. They had long been dealing in gold and silver bullion and in the 1630s, when London merchants began to handle large quantities of Spanish silver, they were drawn more actively into the international exchange market which was shared with bills of exchange* (**125**, **191**). In the domestic market for credit they could dispose of growing resources placed with them for safe-keeping or explicitly for reinvestment. On the latter they could afford to pay interest, and on both kinds of account they could issue their 'bank-note' receipts and accept written 'drafts'*. All these activities are identifiable among the pre-Civil War goldsmiths (**34**).

But the Civil War unquestionably fostered the growth of these functions, and by the 1650s several goldsmiths had conspicuously emerged as large-scale, full-time bankers serving extensive clienteles which included government departments and the state itself. One of these men was Thomas Vyner, or Viner (1588–1665), whose financial services drew honours from the City (as Lord Mayor in 1653), from Cromwell (a knighthood in 1654) and from Charles II (a baronetcy in 1661). Another was Edward Backwell (?1618–1683), briefly a London alderman but never knighted, although his services to the Protectorate and the crown were little inferior to Vyner's. Both men collaborated in some of the major financial operations of the Interregnum and by 1660 they were to prove indispensable to the restoration of Charles II (**33**, **54–5**, **165**).

2 The Reign of Charles II

Charles II thus inherited a legacy of financial principles and practice which had matured considerably beyond those endowed upon his father. During the quarter-century of his reign their evolution was to acquire increasing momentum. There were to be three distinct lines of development:

1 The first was essentially a constitutional process within the public sector which began to shift control of the purse more distinctly towards the House of Commons. It established principles of parliamentary scrutiny of revenue, expenditure and borrowing which were the foundation of all future financial controls (**174**).

2 The second consisted of administrative developments which were potentially in conflict with the first, for they greatly strengthened the machinery of government in general and its financial machinery in particular. The Treasury now emerged, not merely as a distinct department of state but as the dominant one which could sometimes coerce others (**39, 173**).

3 The third occurred within the private sector of the economy, and consisted of an unusually benign set of conjunctures at home and abroad which increased England's prosperity, facilitated its savings and also concentrated its mind upon a more sophisticated system of financial services (**199**).

In each case the processes of change were not smooth or particularly deliberate, but their lines of development were beginning to become interdependent, and any account of them must necessarily move freely between the one and the others.

Perhaps the most disappointing of Charles II's legacies from the Interregnum proved to be the principle of an assured annual income. Intermittent efforts were made in his earliest parliaments to implement the promise of £1.2 million p.a. and additional taxes, such as the hated Chimney Tax of 1662, were introduced to ensure this total. But painstaking modern analysis of Charles II's revenue has shown that, despite these efforts, his ordinary revenues failed to reach their expected target for the first twenty years of the reign (**50**, p. 272).

Wars, trade depression, plague and the Fire of London all contributed to prolonged deficits and the parliaments of the 1660s can be acquitted of any deliberate bad faith. On the contrary, their initial enthusiasm for a strong, restored monarchy made them genuinely eager to ensure that the King could again 'live of his own', free to run his financial affairs as he thought best. They felt it was no business of theirs to scrutinise the financial accounts of the realm or get involved in the routine management of government finance, and when they eventually did it was at the pressing invitation of the King himself.

The Additional Aid of 1665

The crucial initiative which, in the long run, was to help change the whole balance between the crown and Parliament came in 1665. It was a well-meant proposal to facilitate the government's war-time borrowing and it originated with an Exchequer official backed up by the King and Council. The scheme simply required Parliament to guarantee that loans made to the King for the conduct of the Dutch War should be repaid with interest, in strict rotation, out of specially earmarked funds. Lenders were to have official receipts, numbered in sequence and signed by the Lord Treasurer and Chancellor of the Exchequer, which they could (if they wished) sell and assign to others by a written endorsement*. Their 6% p.a. interest, paid half-yearly, was fully guaranteed and repayment from a £1.25 million assessment called 'the Additional Aid' could be expected within two years (**16**, pp. 389–91; **173**, p. 24).

The attractions of this proposal seemed obvious enough. While it still had the old-fashioned overtones of a patriotic 'loyalty loan' it added the practical advantages which investors had learnt to require – 'gilt-edged'* security, a maximum rate of interest and easy transferability. This last element was a truly modern innovation which, it was hoped, would bring England abreast of its European rival, the enemy Dutch. For generations now the Dutch people had been accustomed to invest in a variety of sophisticated, state-guaranteed securities* which included long-term annuities* as well as bearer bonds*, some of which commanded a premium in the open money market (**193**). Nothing like this had yet been seen in England, but with care and good management 'I would lose all I have if it might not easily be brought to this in England, and my Lord I know what I say'. Such was the confidence of the scheme's promoter, Sir George Downing, writing to Charles II's chief minister. As a senior

Exchequer official he was all too familiar with the deficiencies of England's financial administration, and as England's representative at The Hague he was equally acquainted with the merits of the Dutch. His was therefore an authoritative scheme which carried conviction with the King, the Council and, ultimately, with the House of Commons.

However, at least one man possessed sufficient insight to detect its flaws. Edward Hyde, Earl of Clarendon, was in effect prime minister, but as a sick and unpopular man he was badly placed to obstruct Downing once he had secured the King's interest. This failure sours his valuable autobiographical account of the episode [**doc. 3**], yet Clarendon was to be fully justified in believing that Downing's plan was a dangerous step towards parliamentary control of the purse – 'introductive to a commonwealth, and not fit for a monarchy'.

Appropriation*

Earlier parliaments, it is true, had sometimes demanded strict controls over their grants of additional supply. They had done so in the early fifteenth century and most recently, in 1624, had voted for both 'appropriation' (that is, clauses tying the spending of the money to the purpose intended) and 'audit' (provision for a retrospective check that the appropriation had been obeyed) (**16**, pp. 76–80). These, however, were isolated episodes which had conspicuously failed to take root as precedents for control. It was to be very different with Downing's initiative, as Clarendon had feared, for in 1666, to the King's dawning dismay, the principle of appropriation was coupled with a demand for audit, and although the attempt was eventually thwarted it was clear that the genii of parliamentary control had been finally uncorked. Between 1677 and 1679, at the height of a national crisis, Charles was to be faced with appropriation clauses of unparalleled strictness (**16**, p. 396). Even the money lent to the crown was appropriated to the uses intended, thus closing a loophole which had been overlooked in 1665, and the whole campaign to curb the crown's financial autonomy culminated in the resolutions of the House of Commons on 7 January 1681, that anyone who lent money to the government or dealt in government securities without parliamentary authority would be adjudged an enemy to parliaments (**15**, vol. 9, p. 702). The philosophy of accountability which was to shape post-Revolution financial control was thus clearly articulated in the reign of Charles II.

The rate of interest

Meanwhile, looking in another direction, the parliaments of Charles II made a more immediate contribution to financial history. They began to interfere with the rate of interest, authorising preferential rates of 7 and 8% on government borrowing in 1670 and in 1677–79, and thus providing another important precedent for the 1690s. But perhaps most consequential is their re-examination of interest rates in the economy at large. Although in 1660 they had confirmed the Republic's reduction of the legal rate to 6%, this was thought too low by some in 1665 and too high by others in 1668. Contradictory measures were introduced and a brisk debate developed among the pamphleteers. John Locke was encouraged to join in, and although his views on the necessity of letting market forces operate were not published until 1692, his early drafts are a symptom of an increasingly sophisticated understanding of monetary matters (**17**). For, while most people still thought in moral or religious terms about the evils of 'usury'* and the virtues of thrift, some were perceiving that the natural laws of supply and demand would always override man-made constraints on the movement of money and the price for credit. Looking abroad to the Dutch, they could also grasp that uncompetitive domestic rates were a serious burden on trade, for (as Sir George Downing put it):

> this is a certaine maxime, that all trade is govern'd by the rule of Interest of Mony . . . and so, if by reason mony is already at 6 p.Cent at London and but 4 at Amsterdam those of Amsterdam do outtrade those of London, how much more will they be able to out trade them when when they shall pay but 4 at Amsterdam and 8 at London . . . (**171**).

Looking towards home, where the price of land was depressed, another economic expert (the merchant Josiah Child) was equally convinced that 'Land and Interest of Money are, all over the Universe, like two Buckets:. if one go up, the other must go down' (**3, 64**). There were thus dual incentives to secure a reduction of rates by removing the pressures which kept them high. And what were those pressures? A shortage of coin in circulation was generally acknowledged to be one, and Downing's Mint Act of 1666, designed to attract private silver to the Royal Mint for free coinage, was an historic step towards a solution (**81**). But a shortage of currency persisted, particularly in the provinces, and for this there appeared to be an identifiable scapegoat in the London-based goldsmith banker.

'The great reason for want of money in the country is the banker in London,' wrote Sir William Coventry. 'What makes men carry all their money to London but the gain by the Bankers?' argued Sir Edward Seymour; 'Money will never be plentifull till this trade of Bankers be spoiled,' added Sir Thomas Clifford (**12**, vol. 1). These distinguished Members of Parliament, who all held office at the Treasury during their careers, were contributing to the most intensive debate on the English economy to have been mounted since the Restoration. Triggered by the proposal to alter the rate of interest by law as a solution to the post-war experience of boom-and-slump, a House of Lords committee on 'the decay of rents and trade' was set up in 1669 to hear evidence from businessmen and 'experts' alike (**24**, pp. 68–78). Inevitably they all disagreed, but among the arguments which induced the committee to recommend a forced reduction of rates was Josiah Child's evidence on 'the late innovated trade by the bankers in London' (**24**, p. 70).

Thus, although the recommendation was rejected by Parliament, it had helped to stimulate a hostile scrutiny of banks and bankers, and its first effect was a piece of discriminatory taxation upon them in the Subsidy Act of 1670–71 (**24**, pp. 677–8). Designed to tax incomes from offices as well as personal wealth, it noted that 'severall persons being Goldsmiths and others by taking or borrowing great summes of money and lending out the same for extraordinary lucre and profitt have gained and acquired themselves the Reputacon and Name of Bankers' and placed upon them a levy of 15s (or 75p) in every £100 on deposit. Two-thirds of this could be passed on to the banker's private clients, but the measure and its phrasing were a clear expression of the belief that the bankers were profiting unconscionably from the financial necessities of the King and country.

Charles II and his bankers

The belief was not wholly mistaken. Charles in the 1660s was habitually paying his bankers a supplement of 4% above the legal interest rate of 6. This was justifiable: it recognised the special risks run by lenders to a sovereign prince, and was a healthy departure from the practice of his predecessors who had enforced the legal ceiling on their own ill-managed debts. Charles, it might be argued, was taking a creditable step towards a modern market economy by paying the going rate for the crown's very shaky credit [**doc. 2**].

However, to a heavily taxed public the profits which the bankers were believed to be earning were a growing irritant and well-informed observers were not convinced that the liaison between the King and his professional creditors was either healthy or necessary. Downing in particular was convinced that the bankers' monopoly should be broken by a better-managed system of government borrowing solicited directly from the general public. That had been the principal object of his 1665 proposal, and he had been moderately successful, raising nearly £200,000 at only 6% from about 900 subscribers country-wide and putting into circulation over 1,000 Treasury securities (**171**). As Secretary to the Treasury 1667–71 he went on to extend his system, creating printed certificates called 'Treasury Orders', which were legally assignable by endorsement and registered in chronological sequence on the crown's major revenues – Customs, Excise and Chimney Tax [**doc. 4**]. Issued to government departments they were promissory notes upon which the spending departments, such as the Navy, could raise cash in the money market, and when issued to lenders they bore interest at 6% payable half-yearly. Numbered and counter-signed by the Treasury Lords, their date of redemption was advertised by Downing in the weekly *London Gazette*, and they are the direct precursors of the eighteenth-century Exchequer Bill and the Treasury Bills of today.

Yet Downing's efforts to make the Exchequer into a state bank which would rival those of Venice, Genoa or Amsterdam broke down on certain hard facts of English life. One, which requires only a moment's reflection to appreciate, was the physical distance between the Exchequer's offices adjoining Westminster Hall, and the centre of London's financial life which was then, as now, in the City round Lombard Street and Cornhill. Here were the homes of the Royal Exchange (the market for merchants, bills of exchange* and news of all sorts) and of the goldsmith bankers whose 'counters' and strong-room occupied some of the finest houses in post-Fire London. From here to Westminster was a troublesome journey of nearly two miles, cold, wet and dangerous by boat, or muddy and slow through overcrowded streets. That (as Sir John Banks told Pepys on 27 March 1667) was why 'it will be impossible to make the Exchequer ever a true bank to all intents' and Pepys agreed. He also appreciated another reason – the somnolent rituals of the Exchequer, unchanged since the early Middle Ages, unfitted it for modern business requirements. And there was the graver handicap, confided to Pepys by Sir Richard Ford in August 1666 – 'the unsafe condition of a bank under a monarch'. This last weighed heavily with Pepys, who was peculiarly timid in his personal finance, and it was an objection which hampered the development of public borrowing for another generation.

Yet Pepys admired Downing's efforts, and shared his distrust of the bankers, preferring to keep his savings in an iron-bound chest or buried in a country garden (**176**). In this respect he was less than typical of his class or his times, for surviving evidence of the bankers' clientele reveals it to have been widely drawn from government officials and the professions, as well as from merchants, tradesmen and the landed gentry. Analysis of a large sample of Vyner's business in the early 1670s (by then in the hands of a nephew, Sir Robert) suggests that while 7.5 per cent of his clients were titled and 7 per cent were styled 'merchant', the largest groups in ascending order were widows and spinsters (12 per cent), tradesmen (24.4 per cent) and those merely styled 'Esq.' or 'Gent.' (42.7 per cent). Pepys would have found his place among the latter, for they included most of the official class and the professions except the clergy, who represented 2.8 per cent of the clientele. There are famous names among them – Christopher Wren, Robert Boyle, Richard Baxter – and also the less famous but representative names from the well-to-do landed and commercial communities. Inevitably it was largely a London-based clientele, but nearly one-third – holding balances averaging £634 as opposed to the £487 average of the Londoners – had addresses outside the metropolitan area of London and Middlesex, with Yorkshire, Lincolnshire and Wiltshire being as well-represented as the 'home-counties' of the south-east (**171**).

The surviving ledgers of Edward Backwell for 1663–72 confirm this picture. During the six winter months of 1664–65 he held deposits averaging £520 from 1,374 clients, and over the eight years 1664 to 1672 the average total invested with him was £420,000, despite the impact of the Great Fire and the two 'runs' on his bank in 1665 and 1667 (**175**). These deposits, like Vyner's, came from a provincial as well as a London clientele – indeed, nearly one-third of Vyner's depositors had accounts with Backwell or other bankers – and their size and behaviour attest to a well-established 'banking habit' in the moneyed community [**doc. 6**]. They confirm the evidence from other sources that prosperous country gentry, such as the Verneys of Claydon, directed more than one-third of their income from rents towards London for investment or consumption (**66**).

If they invested with Backwell they appear to have had the two classic options – either a non-interest-bearing current account, or a deposit account on which interest terms could be negotiated. There was no advertised market rate. In 1668 the maximum of 6% was conceded to 38 per cent of his clients; 47 per cent were promised 5.5% and the rest could only be sure of 5. The fact that their average deposits were, respectively, £642, £315 and £289 suggests that Backwell was careful to reward the larger investors. Other criteria which he employed very skilfully were the terms of withdrawal – either 'on demand', or 'at 10 days notice', or 14, or 20 or more with the higher rates tending to be granted on the longer terms. Thus, to Sir Thomas Higgons on £50 – 'if it ly more then a mo[nth] to give 6 p.Cent' (**171**, **175**).

But, as in any modern banking system, deposit rates depended ultimately upon the available opportunities for re-investment, and for Backwell and his colleagues in the 1660s these were principally provided by the King and government departments. In September 1664 Backwell had 24 per cent of his assets in loans extended to 558 private customers – merchants, tradesmen, gentlemen. Another 10 per cent was advanced to departmental treasurers, while 63 per cent was tied up in the cycle of loans which he made on the credit of the Customs* revenue. These proportions swung even more heavily in favour of loans to the government during the war of 1665–67 and by 1666 loans to private clients accounted for only 9 per cent of his assets. It becomes clear that Backwell's increasing propensity to grant *all* his depositors the maximum reward of 6% on even short-term notice was directly linked to the opportunities offered by government debts and the assurance of 10% from the King.

To that extent the contemporary case against the goldsmith bankers had foundation. They *did* thrive on the necessities of the nation; they *were* privileged beneficiaries of the King's bounty; they *could* offer unfairly advantageous terms to attract funds from far and wide. The significance of this case is heightened if one appreciates that they were a very small group of fewer than a dozen, and that a less obviously objectionable style of banking was being carried on by their rivals, the heirs to the scriveners.

For, matching the 'big five' goldsmith bankers of the 1660s – Vyner, Backwell, Colville, Snow and the Meynell brothers – was the distinctly different business of Clayton and Morris, to which we have been introduced only recently (**139**). Robert Clayton and John Morris were the business heirs of the Robert Abbott whose substantial operations in the 1650s have been cited already (above, p. 12). In 1658 the deposits placed with their bank fell to £617,710, less than half those of 1652–56, but they rose sharply to £1,380,953 during 1660–63, to £1,515,491 between 1669 and 1672, to £1,763,085 between 1672 and 1675, and reached a peak of £1,828,091 during 1675 to 1677. But few, if any, of these huge resources were reinvested in government securities. Clayton and Morris disdained the Exchequer and concentrated instead upon the ever-active market in mortgages*, on which they were expertly advised by leading specialists in law, estate management and accountancy. They were able to provide for their clients all the usual services of contemporary banking – taking pawns*, offering safe-deposits, honouring drafts*, issuing notes – and also some unusual ones, such as marriage-broking. Indeed, the essence of their business was a broking function – the matching together of well-to-do investors with reliable landed borrowers, whose credentials and securities they submitted to most rigorous scrutinies. Thus, in addition to interest on mortgages issued in their own name, Clayton and Morris did well out of brokerage* and other financial service fees. Unlike the goldsmith bankers, they did not milk the public purse, and this may help to explain the hostility and isolation which surrounded the goldsmith bankers when disaster caught up with them at the end of 1671.

The 'Stop of the Exchequer'

Charles II's decision in December 1671 to defer repayments of his debts was not taken on purely financial grounds. Although his liabilities had risen from the £925,000 he was saddled with at his restoration to nearly £3 million by 1670, the prospects for his peace-time revenue were improving and the debt was steadily diminishing under a programme of retrenchment and land sales (**50**, p. 224). Instead, it was his conspiratorial agreement with Louis XIV to attack the Dutch republic and (perhaps) declare himself a Roman Catholic which determined the timing of this moratorium. The 'Stop', fully implemented in January 1672, was a necessary prelude to the declaration of religious indulgence on 15 March and the declaration of war two days later.

The King's original intention, supported by ministers, was temporarily to free the coming year's revenues from the debt repayments neatly numbered and packaged by Downing's 'Treasury Order' system: it was not an absolute repudiation. Nor was it unpopular. Careful analysis of the debt which was frozen confirms the contemporary belief that most of it was owed to the small circle of goldsmith bankers, and much of that was due for accumulations of interest on old borrowings, not new. Of the £1.3 million that was frozen, nearly 32 per cent was due to Sir Robert Vyner, 22.5 per cent to Edward Backwell, 19 per cent to the Meynells and 6.5 per cent to Colville's successor (**107, 171**). The parliament which met in 1673 showed little sympathy for these bankers and absolutely no inclination to bail out the King. It was therefore left to Charles to protect the bankers who, bombarded with writs from their angry depositors, limped towards bankruptcy in the succeeding decade. Not until 1677 was a solution worked out which did something to appease their creditors and discharge the King. By then, a series of prosperous years following England's disengagement from the Franco-Dutch war of 1672–78 had enabled Charles to fund an annuity* of £140,000 p.a. on the bankers' debt. This they were required to re-allocate to their depositors in the form of 6% annuities, drawn up and witnessed in the Exchequer, authorised under the Great Seal and registered on the securest portion of the royal revenues – the hereditary Excise*. Unwittingly, Charles II had created the first portion of what was to become a permanent 'National Debt' (**107**).

Indeed, these bankers' annuities are of more importance in English financial history than has been generally appreciated, for although involuntarily created, and imposed upon unwilling creditors, they soon evolved into the first long-term investment vehicle of their kind. Careful scrutiny of Exchequer records and of the creditors' wills reveals that they acquired some utility, if not popularity, as a fixed interest security. Some creditors appear to have actually *increased* their debt from the bankers in order to enlarge and round-off their annuity to a more attractive sum. The annuities began to figure in marriage settlements or as endowments for children, and as the prospect for repayment in full began to recede they proved eminently saleable. Six in ten were assigned for value received in their original owner's lifetime (**171**), and although payments of interest faltered and dried up in the 1680s, an active secondary market developed in these annuities which foreshadows the better-known market of the 1690s.

In the 1670s, however, the effect of the 'Stop' was largely destructive, and it figures in English history as a catastrophe little less scandalous than the 'South Sea Bubble'. For there could be no doubt that, in withholding payment on his registered debts, Charles was breaking a solemn promise he had explicitly made in a proclamation of June 1667, at the inception of the Treasury Order system. He thus irreparably damaged the crown's personal credit and brought forward the day when the nation's financial interests would be severed from the private conduct of the sovereign. He also destroyed one generation of bankers. Backwell was insolvent by 1682, Vyner by 1684. Colville's successor collapsed in 1679, and the 'Meynells' heir was in debtors' gaol by 1685. Few of the small circle which had flourished in the 1660s survived to fight again another day (**107**).

After the 'Stop'

Yet their eclipse did not leave a vacuum in government borrowing, for even before 1672 recourse had been possible to several other sources. They fall into three broad categories.

1 First, there were corporate bodies such as the East India Company or the Corporation of the City of London. Possessed of valuable privileges and first-class credit, they were a soft target for coercion, and Charles had no more scruples than his predecessors in putting pressure on them for large-scale loans. The City of London had raised a whole series of loans in the course of the 1660s and the East India Company was likewise repeatedly squeezed for money and goods (**150**). But both bodies began to display increasing disinclination to respond during the 1670s and, thanks to the Fire, the virtual bankruptcy of the City's finance department made it less and less capable to act as lender of last resort. By 1678, when £200,000 was extracted by menaces, the institutional goodwill of the City for the crown had been worn very thin.

2 Then there were the syndicates of revenue 'farmers' who had contracted to collect the Customs*, or the Excise*, or the Chimney Tax, on the government's behalf. Made up of merchants, brewers, bankers and wealthy gentry, these syndicates were gambling on the slim chance that the taxes they had leased might yield them a profit over and above the rental they were pledged to pay the crown. Their fixed-term contracts of between three and seven years, which were won after competitive bidding, generally required them to make substantial advance payments, and it is no surprise to find Vyner and Backwell among the Customs and Chimney Tax syndicates of the 1660s, for few others could assemble sufficient funds. However, some syndicates were profitable enough to generate their own capital, enabling them to mount 'take-over' bids for smaller farms and to emerge as banking groups in their own right. By 1671 a consortium of brewers, already in control of the London and provincial Excise

farms, was on the brink of securing a five-year lease of the Customs and wine duties with an advance of £250,000 and a rental of £600,000 p.a. But their coup was annulled, largely because the government feared an insufferable financial monopoly, and the administration of HM Customs passed under the direct control of the Treasury, where it has remained ever since (**50**). In the case of the Excise and Chimney Tax, however, new groups of lenders continued to emerge during the 1670s, able to raise huge sums in advance and supply a steady flow of loans ahead of revenue receipts. Unfortunately for them, evidence of their substantial profits encouraged the Treasury to impose ever tighter controls and by 1683 the Excise too had been put under direct collection by government officials. Nevertheless, while they had flourished the revenue farms had fostered a new generation of financiers and bankers who worked closely with the third category of fund-raisers, who were indeed the government's own employees.

3 Receivers of revenue (handling government income) and departmental treasurers (handling its expenditure) had in common the fact that large sums of public money passed through their hands and often stuck there for lengthy periods, unaccounted for and available for private reinvestment. Pepys, as treasurer to the garrison at Tangiers, is a minor example of the latter who profited significantly from his opportunities (**176**). Of more significance were successive Treasurers of the Navy and, above all, the Paymaster of the Forces who for much of the reign was Sir Stephen Fox (**56**). It had long been the occupational hazard of such posts that their receipts of cash from the Exchequer would fall short of their obligation to issue pay and settle bills, and in such circumstances office-holders were expected to make ends meet as best they could. They would probably have to borrow, and most of them did, turning to the bankers throughout the 1660s or raising private loans on their personal credit. Yet they rarely lost on their transactions. A banker, who lent them money against an Exchequer IOU at a discount of 10 to 20% was not unwilling to split the difference with them when the Exchequer finally paid up at 100% with interest. That was what Colville was doing for Pepys in August 1666 when the discount on government bills was anything up to 40%. And the Exchequer was willing to grant the treasurers interest in addition to the fees and 'poundage' allowed on their turnover. Skilfully handled, such a system could yield rich returns, and Sir Stephen Fox was outstanding for his success in making it work without incurring the least taint of dishonesty. By

the end of Charles II's reign he had built up a fortune of nearly £240,000 by ploughing back his gains from a prolonged cycle of loans to the Guards and military garrisons and to the royal Household itself (**56**). At the date of 'the Stop' his personal credit was exposed to the tune of £124,000, but he survived unscathed and was able to emerge from the *débâcle* as a major financier in his own right. Between 1674 and 1675 his advances to the government probably exceeded £400,000 at times, and of this as much as £240,000 was borrowed in turn from a wide circle of investors, many of them fellow courtiers and officials. Fox had thus become to all intents and purposes a private banker whose credit reposed ultimately upon the uninterrupted flow of public expenditure.

Similar opportunities were available to the Receivers-General who, during the 1670s, stood as intermediaries between the farmers or collectors of revenues and the Exchequer. Like the treasurers, they too were expected to subsidise government expenditure with short-term loans raised from their own resources, but unlike the treasurers they were well placed to repay themselves from the incoming flows of revenue. This gave them considerable credit in the money market and private investors were as willing to lend to them as they had once lent to the goldsmiths. It was upon these opportunities that there emerged one of the most formidable financiers of late seventeenth-century England. Charles Duncombe (b.?; d. 1711) had been Backwell's apprentice and by 1672 was conducting banking from his master's premises at the sign of the Grasshopper in Lombard Street. He soon became Fox's principal creditor and underwrote Fox's assistant, Richard Kent, who in 1674 became Receiver-General of Excise. This profitable liaison grew, despite Fox's dismissal in 1676, and in 1677 Duncombe and Kent became joint Receivers-General of Customs. By 1680 they were advancing the equivalent of 40 per cent of the government's revenue (**56, 149**).

It is an interesting sidelight on Anglo-Dutch financial relations that in 1678 Prince William of Orange needed to be instructed in the nuances of the English securities market by the future head of the Treasury, Sidney Godolphin [**doc. 7**]. His letters reveal the significant margin between Duncombe's personal credit and that of the Exchequer, as well as the competitive nature of terms offered by other financiers such as Fox, or other countries such as Holland. Duncombe's, it would seem, were the best that England could offer and he was to remain a dominant figure well into the 1690s.

The legacy of Charles II

However, the immediately important point is that, despite 'the Stop', Charles II's reign had fostered several progressive developments in English public finance. Thus it was his quixotic initiative, in appointing the tough-minded Treasury Commission of May 1667, which enabled the Treasury to develop as the most powerful department of government, presiding authoritatively over revenue and expenditure and earning international credit for its efficiency (**39**, **173**). Under capable leaders, such as the Earl of Danby (1673–78) and the Earl of Rochester (1679–87), it became the natural office of the King's 'premier' minister and the stronghold of government patronage. Yet, at the same time, Charles had done much to foster parliamentary control, for despite temptations he had made no serious bid to seek revenues from outside his parliamentary grants. Despite his susceptibility to French subsidies (totalling about £1.165 million), all his major revenues were founded upon the consent of the House of Commons, and the uniquely long life of his 'Cavalier Parliament', sitting from 1661 to 1678, ensured that the principle of appropriation* was able to mature as the key to public credit. Indeed, his 'Stop' of the Exchequer had heavily emphasised the yawning gulf between a trust guaranteed by Parliament and the fragile word of a king. The lessons of 1672 were not to be forgotten. Yet all this had occurred within a context of growing prosperity, healthily reflected in the soaring Customs and Excise yields of the 1670s (**50**). For this too, Charles may be accorded a backhanded kind of credit. It has been said: 'Charles' foreign policy, dishonourable, futile and vacillating as it was, proved no bad thing for trade' (**65**, p. 63), and it is certainly true that his ignominious withdrawal in 1674 from the Franco-Dutch war left England free to pick up the rich prizes of commercial neutrality while her trading rivals fought it out. This interlude of mercantile supremacy in the 1670s, when the full flood of England's colonial produce moved without interruption into receptive European markets, made an invaluable contribution to the formation of capital which was to finance the great wars of the future. The men, the money and the methods which distinguish the conventional epoch of the Financial Revolution can therefore be claimed as the legacy of Charles II.

Visions of reform

Thoughtful subjects of Charles II could have been forgiven for taking a less indulgent view. Dissatisfaction with England's financial practices and institutions was as intense in the 1670s and 1680s as it had been in the 1620s and 1630s, and on much the same grounds. The nation still seemed to lag behind its Continental rivals, lacking as it did cheap credit, universally negotiable* paper and a national banking system. A new generation of pamphleteers arose to reiterate the merits of Dutch, Italian, Spanish or Swedish examples and to explain what could be gained by imitation. For Andrew Yarranton, as for Sir William Petty and many others, the key depicted in his pamphlet of 1679, *England's Improvement by Sea and Land, To Out-do the Dutch without Fighting, To Pay Debts without Moneys, To set at work all the Poor of England* . . ., was a banking system secured upon publicly registered land-values. The idea was not novel. Plans for a comprehensive Land Registry had been vigorously promoted in the 1650s and were to reach their height in the 'Land Bank' schemes of the 1690s (**108**). Other schemes sought to capitalise on the values locked away in commercial goods. Huge warehouses or 'Lumbards' were envisaged in which traders' deposits of non-perishables could be pawned for between two-thirds and four-fifths of their value, realised not in cash but in short-term 'bills of credit' costing perhaps 3 or 4% p.a. The details of these schemes varied and were often imprecise and impracticable, but running through all of them in the 1670s is an urgent desire to see paper-money and bank-credits supplement the inadequate coinage and so liberate the productive energies of the nation. 'Then there would be as great a Bank at London as at Amsterdam . . . and as great a Bank at Bristol as at Hamburgh . . . And as great a Bank at Exeter as at Noremberge. . . .'

Such a regeneration of provincial England was the common objective of several writers, and both Francis Cradocke and his imitator, Dr Mark Lewis, envisaged a country divided into several hundred banking 'precincts', each served by a note-issuing deposit bank. The latter's notion of locally elected bank managers and directors (one vote per £10 of customer's income), may seem preposterous, but his anticipation of 'marbled paper' bank-notes (to foil forgers), of inter-bank transfers (to thwart highwaymen) and of bank profits invested in local services such as hospitals, strikes a more interesting note. Social amelioration, in a community where it was reckoned that half the population lived at or below subsistence level, is an unsurprising feature of many such schemes.

Inevitable also is the role accorded to London, with its centre and environs holding about a tenth of the population and much of its wealth. Several planners sought the collaboration of the City's

Corporation, and on 29 August 1682 the Lord Mayor and Aldermen signed a draft agreement for 'the Bank of Credit of the City of London'. Given wide publicity by pamphlets such as *Corporation Credit* and *England's Interest*, it boasted of wealthy backers and solicited subscriptions at half a dozen City and West-End coffee-houses, but it appears to have been eclipsed by a more imaginative plan set up by a group of leading merchants and Members of Parliament who proposed to engraft their bank upon the corporate privileges possessed by the nearly defunct 'Royal Fishery Company' (**183**, vol. 3, pp. 202–3). In their search for joint-stock institutional security, centred upon London, these men were groping their way towards a new kind of bank, of the sort which was to emerge in the 1690s.

But 1682 was an inauspicious time at which to launch such enterprises, particularly in London. For it was in this year of booming revenues and growing financial independence that Charles II was able to round upon his political enemies and take his considered revenge for the bitter 'exclusion' campaigns that had been mounted against his Roman Catholic brother's right to succeed him on the throne. London 'Whigs', drawn heavily from the business community, had been at the forefront of these campaigns, and it was against their stronghold in the City's government that Charles directed his attack. By October 1683, after lengthy legal proceedings, the City's corporate privileges were adjudged to be forfeit. The leading London Livery Companies suffered a similar fate, and the City's corporate institutions were submitted to a forcible reconstruction which replaced its leaders with reliable 'Tories'. There thus commenced a new social and financial antagonism in English history, couched in the novel political language of the 1680s. It was to sour the course of the Financial Revolution for many years to come.

For, although the wealth of London was far from being a 'Whig' monopoly, it possessed the timeless propensity of all capital – to fear violence, to hate uncertainty and to distrust the reliability of strong but autocratic government. Although trade continued to flourish in Charles's last years there is some evidence of flights of capital, as well as of Whigs, to Amsterdam and Hamburg, and in this climate of political tension there was little chance that the teeming visions and ambitious schemes of the 1670s and 1680s would reach fulfilment.

Part Two: 1685–1714

3   Revolution and Revolutions

The reign of James II

In 1680 the future James II had expressed relish for the growing financial independence of his brother, for 'now that his Ma[jesty] is able to subsist upon his own revenu[e], without the help of a Parliament' he foresaw that 'in a short tyme he will be as much master, as he was presently after his restoration'. In 1683 likewise he exulted in the forfeiture of London's privileges: 'this has been a great day for the monarchy' (**22**, pp. 513, 577). Such remarks seem to augur ill for the future of parliamentary control of finance and the development of a progressive London money market. They confirm the assumption, which is deeply rooted in all interpretations of the financial revolution, that none of it could have happened but for the removal of James II in 1688.

That assumption may be unwise. The history of French public finance in the seventeenth and eighteenth centuries (and, indeed, that of Austria) does not demonstrate that banking, borrowing and fiscal ingenuity were wholly incompatible with autocratic government by a Roman Catholic monarchy (**73**, **167**). Nor did the accession of James immediately stifle the financial innovations and institutions of his brother's reign. On the contrary, the small circle of financiers and courtiers who were underwriting the last years of Charles II was equally supportive of James II, and it was not until November 1688 that Duncombe, finally despairing of his master, abandoned him for the service of the incoming regime (**112**). As for Parliament, when it sat in 1685 it faced no obstacles in incorporating the complete structure of Downing's system of assignable*, registered Treasury Orders into its 8% loan authorisation for £400,000 (1 Jac. II, c.5, clauses vii–ix).

However, it is idle to speculate what might have been the future for England's financial institutions if James and his descendants had reigned for the full span of their natural lives. They were not allowed to do so, and the wars which barred their return had profoundly dramatic effects upon the nature of Parliament, taxation, borrowing and banking.

James II's short reign made some contribution to these changes but the contribution was negative: it demonstrated what was *not* acceptable, what could *not* be permitted to happen again. This was particularly true of the financial settlement which inaugurated his reign. James did not wait for the formalities of parliamentary consent before collecting the same revenues which had been endowed upon his brother's life, and all that was left for his first Parliament was, after slight hesitation, to give assent to an accomplished fact. Obeying his injunction to 'use me well' it did more, adding to Customs, Excise and Chimney Tax a group of additional, short-term duties which in due course brought his total revenues above £2 million p.a. It has been argued that this outcome was not wholly intentional and certainly not reckless (**51**). The House of Commons had no means of foreseeing the continuing trade-boom which by 1687–88 had increased tax-yields by a third above those of 1683–84. Seeking only to pay off the crown's debts and meet the costs of defeating Monmouth's and Argyll's rebellions, the Parliament of 1685 had honourably done its duty and nothing more. However, this bland acquittal does not quite square with the misgivings expressed by some MPs in the sparsely recorded debates of November 1685. These reveal a dawning sense of alarm at the generosity of their grants, from which two consequences were foreseen – first, that James might have no further use for Parliaments, and second, that he was now able to maintain a standing army twice as large as that of Charles II (**52**). Only a handful of veteran MPs had time to express those fears in November 1685 before an abrupt closure put an end to their sitting (**12**, vol. 5). They did not meet again under James.

The financial settlement, 1689–90

Against this immediate background it is easier to understand the extraordinary features of the financial settlement which was imposed upon William III. For although it was again agreed in principle that the crown should enjoy revenues totalling £1.2 million p.a. the Parliaments of 1689 and 1690 were determined not to repeat the mistakes of 1685 or, indeed, of 1660. In speech after speech MPs revealed their conviction that they and their predecessors had been too lax with Charles, too generous with James. Argued one MP, 'Our greatest misery was, our giving [the revenue] to King James for life.' Another, 'If King Charles had not had that bounty from you, he had never attempted what he had done.' A House of

Commons, filled with experienced members, two-thirds of whom had sat in earlier Parliaments, needed little convincing. Whether Whig or Tory, the lessons they had learned were clear enough: 'When Princes have not needed Money, they have not needed us' [**doc. 8**]. But, providentially, James II's flight had placed a remedy within their reach, and a series of speeches revealed a new kind of constitutional pragmatism which is best conveyed in their own words. Thus, it was pointed out, 'You have an infallible security for the administration of the Government: All the Revenue is in your own hands, which fell with the last King, and you may keep that back. Can he whom you place on the Throne support the Government without the Revenue?' Another warned: 'I think we ought to be cautious of the Revenue, which is the life of the Government, and consider the two last Reigns. If you give this Revenue for three years you will be secure of a Parliament.' 'But', added another, 'if you leave the thing indefinite, you will have, I believe, little or no use of a Parliament for the future.'

Arguments such as these, developed over the twelve months of 1689, reflect a protracted but consistent line of reasoning which by 1690 had placed parliamentary control of government finance at the cornerstone of the constitution. For, although it took much time and considerable agonising to reach agreement, it became abundantly clear that no Triennial Act (requiring regular parliaments), no annual Mutiny Act (ensuring army discipline), no Declaration of Rights and, perhaps, no Magna Carta, could be a more effective guarantee of parliamentary monarchy and the rule of law than effective control of the sovereign's purse. With great deliberation William and Mary were thus *not* endowed with an assured revenue for life. The main Customs revenue of 'tonnage and poundage', worth an estimated £577,507 p.a., was eventually granted them, but for only four years in the first instance and it was soon allocated to specific heads of expenditure, as were even the hereditary revenues of the crown. It was conceded as a general principle that £600,000 of the crown's notional income should be reserved for civil government, as opposed to military expenditure, but even this proviso – the historic origin of the 'Civil List' – was negated by the weight of old debts and new charges placed upon it (**163**). In brief: 'three features distinguish the financial settlement of 1690: it was temporary, it was inadequate and it was encumbered' (**168**).

Some MPs had the grace to be ashamed of the paradox (which deeply embittered William) that 'a Prince, come to save your Religion and Laws' should be rewarded with so much less generosity

31

than James II, who had sought to destroy both. It was pointed out that William 'has trusted you with all he has in the World'; 'the King, I may say, has robbed himself to supply the Public'. Indeed, in a well-meant but futile gesture of goodwill William had voluntarily surrendered the much-hated Chimney Tax, worth over £200,000 p.a., and in addition £600,000 was still owing for the huge Dutch military effort on England's behalf. Yet arguments such as these, though they cut deep, could not obscure a more profound perception, that in future government finance should no longer be exclusively tied to the person of the sovereign. The crown's revenue was now to be thought of as a public revenue: 'it is in the crown as a Trust' and 'what is given to the King . . . is not as he is King, but for support of the Nation, to take care of it'. The revenue settlement of the Glorious Revolution therefore marks an important stage in constitutional transition from a convention of financial deference to a sovereign ruling by divine right towards a much more pragmatic treatment of the reigning monarch as a tenured executive, a public servant 'kept as it were at Board wages'. Parliament, and above all the House of Commons, which paid the piper, would henceforth call the tune. 'We that have placed the King on the Throne, are those that will keep him in it.' And the future strategy of parliamentary supply was brutally simple: 'If you give the crown too little, you may add at any time; if once you give too much, you will never have it back again' (**12**, vols 9, 10).

Coming as they did from two former Speakers of the House of Commons (the Tory Sir Edward Seymour and the Whiggish Sir William Williams respectively) these last two statements carried a high degree of non-partisan authority and they go far towards justifying the argument of Professor Clayton Roberts that the financial constraints imposed upon William III were essential elements in a deliberate constitutional strategy, and not mere incidental by-products of a war-time emergency (**168**). However, the fact that William's accession immediately plunged England into the most costly war it had ever faced is fundamental to understanding the other major features of the financial revolution – the proliferation of new taxes, the raising of huge loans and the creation of new institutions such as the Bank of England and the market in stocks and shares.

4 The Financing of War

Taxation

England fought the Nine Years War (1688–97) principally in Ireland, Flanders and in European waters – a modest strategic commitment by later standards but of a scale not experienced since the vainglorious French campaigns of Henry VIII. It required an army of up to 90,000 men and a seagoing force of over 40,000. Add to these the cost of new shipping, subsidies to Continental allies and the supplies of a large overseas force and it is easy to comprehend the total cost averaging £5.5 million p.a. (**118**).

This posed a terrifying dilemma to a Parliament of landowners who, to be fair to them, were not wholly indifferent to the interests of England's commerce, industry and common people. Where was the tax burden to be placed? Upon capital or upon incomes? On consumption or production? Upon imports or exports? Luxuries or necessities? Upon land or . . . upon what? At a time when trade was seriously curtailed by French privateering and consumption crippled by rising prices the options available for taxation were shrinking daily and the House of Commons' debates on 'ways and means' of financing the war were often agonised. They taxed coaches and London property development (to soak the rich) but taxed salt and burdened beer (which hurt the poor). Wine, spirits and tobacco, tea and coffee were all brought under contribution, and births, burials, bachelors and marriage did not escape. These piecemeal measures reflect a deep aversion to a comprehensive 'general Excise' on all retailed commodities, which MPs feared would too easily become a seductively large and irremovable burden. In preference to that nightmare they turned reluctantly to levies on wealth and status. But their Poll taxes were highly unpopular and their attempts to administer an annually re-assessed tax upon wealth and incomes yielded diminishing returns. Their levy of 4s in the £ raised £1.92 million at its best in 1693, but only £1.66 million at its worst in 1697. In 1698 it was therefore decided to abandon the annual assessments and take the 1693 yield and distribution as a fixed quota to be shared out among the counties. In this manner 'the Land Tax' – as it was incorrectly called – came into being as a reliable, annual resource, leviable according to need at between 1s and 4s in the £ (**40**, **194**, **196**). Between 1689 and 1700 these assessed taxes produced over 39 per cent of government income, compared with under 24 per cent from Customs and under 26 per cent from Excise.

Borrowing

Yet even these strenuous fiscal exertions could not cover the the immediate costs of the war, and from the outset it was necessary to borrow, using all the standard techniques of the past. The Receivers of Customs and Excise were again called upon for large cash advances, the general public was wooed with offers of 7 or 8% and the Corporation of the City of London, restored to its privileges, advanced more than a quarter of the loans raised on the credit of parliamentary taxes between 1689 and 1693. However, these were short-term loans which presupposed early repayment from reliable funds. But the funds, ingenious though they were, often proved unreliable and the government securities* registered upon them began to change hands at larger and larger discounts*, thus forcing the real cost of public borrowing well above the formal rate of interest.

Contemporaries called these government securities 'tallies' after the time-hallowed wooden laths which (when cut with a graduated series of notches to indicate 1000s, 100s, 10s of £s and smaller cuts for shillings and pence, inscribed on both sides in Latin words and roman numerals and then slit down the middle to create foil and counter-foil) served in the Exchequer as forger-proof receipts. They were issued to tax-collecting officials for their payments and to the public in return for cash loans, but they were more commonly distributed in large numbers and convenient denominations to government departments for payments and loans yet to be made. Departmental treasurers thus acted as secondary issuers of Exchequer tallies which they hawked around the money market in search of cash or pressed upon contractors and employees for goods and services. However, accompanying these awkward wooden sticks was a more modern paper instrument, the printed Treasury Order introduced in the 1660s. Bearing the same information as the tally but in English words and arabic numerals, numbered in chronological sequence, registered for payment from a specific revenue and validated by official signatures, these were the government securities which the general public also chose to call 'tallies' [**doc. 4**]. But, unlike the sticks, they could be easily endorsed and transferred by a written assignment, which allowed them to circulate freely until their date of redemption* at the Exchequer came round – an event duly advertised in *The London Gazette*. It was these 'tallies' which now glutted the market, bringing cries of distress from the trades-men, merchants and departmental officials who held them but could raise no money upon them except at discounts of 25 to 35 per cent. By the end of 1692 the Treasury Lords were reporting to the House of Commons that 'the Exchequer was never barer than now' and 'the Treasury at this time is very low; there is hardly money to pay the army their weekly subsistence money' (**13**, pp. 230, 283).

Facing a critical situation, the government had to adopt unusual remedies. It turned in desperation to three devices for which there were successful foreign examples – namely, lotteries, tontines and annuities. All appealed to the gambling instinct by injecting a larger chance of a windfall into the normal rewards of lending. Thus, the 'Million Lottery' of 1694 offered 100,000 tickets at £10, the least of which would win £1 p.a. for 16 years and the best £1,000 p.a., paid for from salt and liquor duties. A year earlier the £1 million 'tontine' was launched: subscribers could buy the right to nominate a 'life', that is, a person who, if he or she survived, would bring the investor a return of 10% p.a. until 1700 and then an increasing share of £70,000 divided among the survivors over the next ninety-nine years. For less optimistic subscribers the scheme offered an alternative, a 14% annuity on their own lives, and in the event nearly all the £1 million was subscribed for this generous option (**72**, pp. 52–4).

Creating a financial liability on the public purse which would last for nearly a century, the tontines and annuities of 1693 mark the start of deliberate long-term borrowing* in English history – an event of great significance but one which has been eclipsed by another momentous innovation – the foundation of the Bank of England in 1694.

The Bank of England

Throughout the seventeenth century the argument for the foun-dation of a national bank or banks had been intermittently put for-ward by numerous publicists. Yet until 1692 the case had never been sympathetically considered in Parliament. On the contrary, the landowning governing class had little love for 'moneyed men'. To them banks meant usury, debts and foreclosures. Worse still, with memories of the 1660s, they could mean furtive support for an un-scrupulous king. Deep prejudices had to be overcome to allow the House of Commons even to consider the proposal which was raised on 12 January 1692, 'that a public bank might be established for taking up of money'. In the event the House only agreed to appoint a committee 'to receive proposals for a fund of perpetual interest in order to the raising a sum of money for carrying on the war against France' [**doc. 9**]. But in response to this signal a whole swarm of banking schemes emerged like bees from their authors' bonnets, con-fusing the public with a bewildering variety of alternatives (**108**). Surprisingly, one of the first came from some of the owners of those 'Bankers annuities' created to appease the victims of the 1672 'Stop'. They were said to be willing to lend another £1 million at 5% if only their annuities, not fully paid since 1683, would be properly honoured (**13**, p. 135). But their case was *sub judice* and the govern-ment passed on to less embarrassing ideas. Some offered tontines, others large-scale mortgages; most envisaged the issue of paper cur-rency and all involved the long-term appropriation of future revenue to the payment of interest. But for how long? A fixed term, or per-petual? And how much? Should it be at 5% or 6, or 7, or even 8%? And should the bank's notes be legal tender or merely payable for taxes? And what was in it for the shareholders and managers? After two years spent revolving these options the scheme finally adopted is credited to William Paterson, a pertinacious and prolific Scottish 'projector' who was author of many financial tracts (**2**). But he had no magic formula; the essential ideas of his proposal were common-place and the Act of Parliament of April 1694 which inaugurated the Bank was a nervous compromise devised by the Chancellor of the Exchequer, Charles Montagu. The Act pledged taxes on ship-ping and liquors to a total of £140,000 p.a. of which £100,000 would reward subscribers of a £1.2 million loan with 8% p.a. and the man-agement with £4,000 p.a.; the rest would service the purchasers of £300,000-worth of annuities. Pessimistically, the Act allowed that even if only half the hoped-for £1.2 million were subscribed by 1 August 1694 it would qualify the contributors for incorporation under royal charter as 'the Governor and Company of the Bank of England', with a tenure assured until 1706.

In the event, as every schoolboy used to know, the sub-scription* was rapidly filled. Opening on 21 June and headed by the King and Queen, the list of 1,268 subscribers was completed by 2 July. The promised charter was sealed on 27 July and the

Bank of England was immediately in business (**53**).

Yet the business undertaken by what was often called in its early days 'the Bank of London' bore little resemblance to the services expected of a modern 'central' bank or a 'high-street' bank or even those provided by other seventeenth-century bankers. The early Bank of England has been variously described as 'a money raising machine' or 'an investment trust', singlemindedly limited to lending £1.2 million to the government. This it quickly did, but in paper, not in coin. For, until the autumn of 1694, only 25 per cent of the subscription had to be paid up in cash; 35 per cent more would be due by November, but in any case what had been created by incorporation* was something more precious than cash, and that was credit. Thus the Bank's 'sealed bills', in which it paid the Exchequer £1.2 million in convenient denominations of £100, represented so much credit – not cash – as did the Exchequer 'tallies' which it got in return. Indeed, it was this creation of credit, in the form of circulating paper, which had been the paramount objective of the scheme, and in this respect the Bank was an immediate success. It soon began to issue paper to its depositors, allowing them the choice of either an account book, or a loose-leaf receipt note, or 'a running cash note' payable to the named depositor or 'to bearer'. Printed notes of this last category were engraved in denominations of £5, £10, £20, £50 and £100 and, although not at first issued for fear of counterfeiting, they mark the genesis of the familiar Bank of England note with its characteristic 'Promise to pay ... the bearer on demand' (**93**, p. 23).

Thus although the Bank, sited initially in the premises of the Grocers livery company, offered a range of personal services such as holding deposits, taking pawns* and discounting bills of exchange*, its principal client remained the government, and in the early years of its life it sought to justify its existence by a series of major services to the state [**doc. 11**]. From the start it continued to lend to the Treasury, controversially in excess of its authorised capital. More daringly, it undertook the remittance of funds to the British forces fighting in Flanders. Working against a deteriorating exchange rate this proved very unprofitable, and it also cost the life of a leading Bank director, Michael Godfrey, who was killed on a visit to the trenches. As it was, the Bank had to borrow heavily from the Dutch, but its operations were a useful loss-leader which earned the gratitude of the government at a critical stage of the war. This in turn enabled the Bank to survive two other crises which have an important place in the financial revolution.

The great recoinage of 1696

One was 'the great recoinage' of 1696–99, an immense operation of great risk and doubtful wisdom which exercised some of the best minds of the age – Isaac Newton, John Locke, Christopher Wren, William Lowndes and many others (**129**). The problem to be solved was the serious and growing deterioration of England's silver coinage. Not merely was it old and worn, it was being deliberately clipped away to produce small parings for melting down and sale as bullion, most of which was exported. This practice bred multiple adverse effects. The silver coins in circulation lacked 40 to 50 per cent of their original weight, while full-weight coins were being hoarded, melted or smuggled away. The consequent shortage raised prices; golden guineas (with milled edges less vulnerable to clipping) rose in value and a complex, accelerating distortion of England's trade balance, exchange rates and domestic economy followed (**23**, pp. 698–701; **118**, pp. 20–2; 245–7).

To tackle this problem at the height of a costly war was indeed to mend one's roof in a thunderstorm, yet it had to be done, and after bitter disagreements among the experts it was done in the most painful of ways. For instead of devaluing as Newton and Lowndes recommended, so that the silver content of the new coinage would differ little from that of the old, clipped pieces, it was decided to re-coin at the old high standard (as Locke insisted), so that it would take roughly two clipped shillings to produce the silver needed for one new one. By the terms of the Recoinage Act of 1696 under-weight coins could be accepted at their face value only for tax payments up to 4 May and for government loans up to 24 June; after these dates old coins would be valued by weight, leaving those too poor to pay taxes or too slow to make loans bearing a substantial loss (**108**, **129**).

The Bank of England was not directly involved in this brutal exercise, but on 6 May, as customers clamoured for the new, full-weight coins, it faced up to its first 'run' and was obliged to suspend payment on its notes. This was a blow to its infant credit just when it was facing the second of its major crises – the birth of a potential rival.

The Land Bank

The idea of a bank whose collateral security would consist of registered lands had been around for many years. Essentially it envisaged large-scale mortgages*, but whereas modern home-buyers capitalise on their future income to acquire property, Land Bank subscribers were to capitalise their property to acquire future income, much of it in the form of transferable, interest-bearing paper. This had many attractions. Land was stable, durable, visible and unlike gold and silver, which shared these merits, it was undeniably English. These were attributes which greatly appealed to patriotic country gentlemen and gave the Land Bank notion a social and political significance which set it apart from its alien rivals [**doc. 12**]. In 1695 at least three such schemes were launched with influential backing and in February 1696 the two most successful agreed to collaborate. In April they secured parliamentary incorporation* as 'the Governor and Company of the National Land Bank' and posed an unequivocal challenge to the Bank of England. Their Act of incorporation guaranteed their investors a return of 7% p.a. on a loan to the government of £2.564 million, half of which had to be subscribed by 1 August (**108, 179**).

But the enthusiasms of July 1694 were not matched in July 1696, and the subscription* was a pitiful failure. Only three subscribers appeared with a total of £2,100, and within a few weeks the field was again clear for the Bank of England to assert its dominant role. It consolidated its ascendancy by undertaking to absorb another £1 million of government 'tallies' and was rewarded in 1697 by a substantial extension of its powers. Forgery of its notes was made punishable by death (as if they were coin of the realm); its charter was prolonged until 1711, and it was guaranteed that no rival corporate bank would be allowed to emerge.

Grateful for this reprieve the Bank's directors undertook a further service to the state. They agreed to support the introduction of another distinctive product of the financial revolution – the 'Exchequer bill'*. In direct line of descent from Downing's Treasury Orders, Charles Montagu's Exchequer bills of 1696 were printed, numbered notes, promising interest at 3d per day per £100, but were issued in convenient units of £5 and £10 (**72**, pp. 365–7). They were designed to alleviate the shortage of circulating currency during the great recoinage, but they were not an immediate success, so in 1697 a consortium of the Bank's directors undertook, in their personal capacities, to underwrite the circulation of the bills – in return for a generous allowance. Thereafter the bills, which were recycled back to the Exchequer at the end of a year, appear to have entered into general circulation, adding to the volume of paper currency, easing the government's liquidity* and playing an increasingly important part in the Bank of England's operations (**53, 72**).

Thus, leaning wearily upon each other, the Bank of England and William III's government managed to stagger through to the peace of October 1697. It had been a close-run thing – just how close has only recently been assessed (**118**). With England's resources doubly squeezed, by huge external drains of funds at a time of near-collapse in overseas earnings, there is irony in the revelation by Dr D. W. Jones that only the export of illegal silver clippings kept England's war-effort afloat through the early 1690s (ibid., p. 228). Yet this does not invalidate another expert verdict, that:

> in view of [the Bank of England's] services to the stability of public finance and the improvement of public borrowing from the year of its foundation no other institution contributed more to the stability of the Revolution settlement or underwrote more effectively the liberties that Englishmen enjoyed (**74**, p. 289).

The politics of finance

In the 1690s and beyond, some Englishmen would have profoundly disagreed with that Whiggish encomium. Whether as Tories, or Anglicans, country gentlemen or advocates of Land Banks (and they were often all four) they would have invoked social, political, economic and religious grounds for articulating a deep hostility to the Bank and all it stood for.

From the start, the Bank of England had had its critics. The passage of its founding Act had been opposed in both Houses of Parliament and significant amendments had been inserted to prevent the Bank from subverting the constitution. It was not to lend money to the crown or buy crown lands without parliamentary consent, and its management could not be discharged of wrongdoing by the mere will of the King. But, as the social and political characteristics of the Bank became clearer these Whiggish precautions were superseded by 'country-Tory' resentments. Indeed, modern analysis of the Bank's subscribers and directorate confirms the contemporary perception that it was a predominantly Whig institution, with strong nonconformist affiliations and narrowly drawn from a metropolitan, 'bourgeois' base (**68**).

As their names suggest – Janssen, Denew, Lethieullier and no less than three Houblons – several of the Bank's earliest directors were of immigrant origin (as, indeed, was 'James Bateman'). They and their colleagues were, for the most part, leaders of London's merchant aristocracy, possessed not merely of great wealth but often of civic offices or parliamentary seats and multiple director-ships of the great trading companies. Several had records of political opposition to James II and had suffered for it; several were champions of religious dissent. Inevitably such men had enemies, for they seemed to embody the most disturbing characteristics of a rapidly changing society – alien, disloyal, nonconforming *arrivistes* who exalted the values of mere money above those of land and rank.

That descriptive travesty acquired some plausibility from certain observable features of the 1690s. For a start, the dissenting interest *did* exercise a disproportionately large influence in London's life. Accounting for barely 20 per cent of its population, dissenters appear to have provided over 27 per cent of the City's short-term loans between 1689 and 1691, and, while between 18 to 25 per cent of the Bank of England's original subscribers had traceable dissenting con-nections, dissenters account for over 40 per cent of the Bank's directors (**68**). Politically, their affiliations were overwhelmingly Whig, and it was Whigs who dominated the civic authority of Lon-don in the 1690s. Contemporary observers who may have lacked this statistical assurance nonetheless had a clear picture of collusion between a financial-political oligarchy in the City and an increas-ingly partisan government. And, like any government, this one could be blamed for many things: for a mismanaged war effort, for waste and corruption and, above all, for high and inequitable tax-ation. Carefully contrived though it was to tax all kinds of wealth, the 'Land Tax' at 4s in the £ bore heavily upon its well-to-do victims. For example, the immensely wealthy Sir John Banks (1627–99), who had cheerfully borne levies of 4 to 5 per cent on his rentals in the 1660s, felt this burden rise from 16 to 27 per cent in the course of the 1690s (**59**). Fortunately, as an experienced finan-cier as well as a landed magnate, he knew how to offset these charges with lightly taxed gains on government loans, but for mere land-owners the burden was severe and unrelieved. It was out of their consequent sense of injustice that a shared sense of identity was born. 'The landed interest', carrying up to 50 per cent of the annual tax burden of the war, began to discover itself in the 1690s and in doing so unmasked its imaginary adversary – 'the monied interest' (**71**, **91**, **102**, **184**).

The birth of the stock market

Nothing did more to confirm the belief in a sinister 'monied interest' than the development of the London market for stocks* and shares*. Although a formal Stock Exchange, with exclusive premises and institutional rules, did not emerge until late in the eighteenth century (**144**), its origins as a market are clear enough, for by the 1690s it possessed not merely a physical location in the alleys between Cornhill and Lombard Street [**doc. 14**] but also a distinct community with its own language, its own rules and its own values. More than any other feature of the financial revolution, the stock market is the most characteristic product of the 1690s. True, there had been a market for stocks and a market for money well before 1688. The arcades of the Royal Exchange (rebuilt in 1669) and the taverns and coffee houses nearby had for long offered locations where deals could be sought and agreements concluded. Bill-brokers, money-brokers and insurance-brokers had their known 'walks' and pitches and news from every quarter of the trading world had its customary time and place of communication. Speculation within the Royal Exchange concentrated mainly on commodities, for by 1675 there were over 300 items quoted in the London 'price-currents' and nearly 500 in Amsterdam's (**160**). European exchange rates also figured importantly in these weekly, printed lists – but stock prices only rarely, for there were only a handful of eligible joint-stock* companies and of these only the East India Company's stock was quoted with any frequency. Although sophisticated observers of the European economy, such as Downing, had advised studying the movements of the Dutch East India Company's stock as 'the pulse of the country', it was long before the same could be said of its English rival. Likewise, the average annual turnover in the stock of the Royal African Company, floated in 1671 with 200 subscribers and £110,000 in capital, was only about £16,000, and no other stocks offered a truly speculative market (**65, 183**).

Yet Charles II's last years had seen a brisk stirring of enterprise, and Defoe, writing in the 1690s, had no hesitation in naming 1680 as the year which saw the real birth of 'the art and mystery of projecting' (**7**, p. 25). By 'projecting' he meant invention, enterprise or company promotion and the 1680s certainly saw a trickle of all three which, measured by the number of new patents enrolled, became an astonishing flood between 1691 and 1693. However, economic historians have been warned not to mistake the sixty-one patents registered in these years for a boom in genuine invention or technical change (**131**). They reflect a wave of speculative excitement fed by the liberation of risk capital and the example set by a few exceptionally lucrative stocks. A wreck-salvage investment had returned several thousand per cent; East India Company dividends totalled 420 per cent between 1680 and 1691, and various utility companies for water and lighting had made auspicious beginnings (**183**). In their wake came a flock of schemes, some sound, some feeble and some fraudulent, which moved the anonymous author of *Angliae Tutamen* to his diatribe in 1695 [**doc. 13**]. By then dealings were possible in nearly 140 English and Scottish companies and a viable stock market was coming into being, served by brokers and jobbers and reported by a financial press.

John Houghton's *Collections for Improvement of Husbandry and Trade* began life in March 1692 as a weekly devoted to useful knowledge of a bucolic kind – the virtues of manure, turnips, cider and pancakes – but by its ninety-ninth issue it had discovered the excitements of stocks and shares and set out to explain to its readers the alien language and arcane rituals of financial speculation [**doc. 10**]. The fact that it began its lessons with the sophisticated process of dealing in 'options' is surprising but reveals just how fast the infant market had developed by 1694. Before long, John Castaing's *Course of the Exchange*, listing the current prices for Bank, East India Company and African Company stock as well as the status of Exchequer loans in the process of repayment, had become a regular publication. He was assured of an avid readership and his weekly lists became in due course the official record of the modern Stock Exchange. However, not all public comment was as impartial as this. As early as January 1692 a veteran Tory MP had exploded in wrath against the mushrooming market: 'the trade of stockjobbing is now become the sole business of many, which has ruined great numbers . . . ' (**13**, p. 147). It was the start of a parliamentary reaction which in 1697 produced an Act restricting the number of all City brokers to 100 and their fees to one-eighth of a per cent. But broking – strictly the introduction by a neutral middleman of buyer and seller – was not the problem. It was 'jobbing' – the speculative dealing and manipulation of a security by a dealer who might, or might not, own it, which was under attack. Defoe was to pour a torrent of abuse upon the practice – 'founded in Fraud, born of Deceit, and nourished by Trick, Cheat, Wheedle, Forgeries, Falshood' – and upon the practitioners – 'meer original Thieves and Pick-Pockets' who could ruin men 'by the strange and unheard of Engines of Interests, Discounts, Transfers, Tallies, Debentures, Shares,

Projects and the Devil and all of Figures and hard names' (**8, 10**).

Behind the smoke of this invective glimmered the fire of a genuine grievance, for Defoe – himself an undischarged bankrupt – was not alone in hating this new world of easy money and easier virtue. There was soon a record of notorious financial scandal, chicanery and crime in high places to support his case. Bribery was exposed in the Treasury, and fraud was proved in the Exchequer (**39**). In 1698 the Cashier of the Customs and the Cashier of the Excise (who was still Charles Duncombe) were accused of forgery and fraud and expelled from the House of Commons. There were to be too many such accusations and rather too few convictions in the early years, with the result that the smell of financial corruption soon settled like a cloud upon this novel world of fast profits and overnight fortunes. Never before in English history had so much money passed so quickly through so many hands and, inevitably, some of it stuck as it passed.

Because so much was now at stake in material terms, the contest for political, commercial and financial advantage acquired an unparalleled intensity in these years. The abortive launch of the National Land Bank was only one symptom of the struggle. It was accompanied by a longer, more bitter battle between the largely Tory directors of the East India Company and their largely Whig rivals who, in 1698, secured their own incorporation as 'the New East India Company' with a promise of a £2 million loan to the state (**110**). Supported by the same magnates who were backing the Bank of England, the new company seemed to consolidate the ascendancy of the new men and the new money which made up 'the monied interest'. It mattered not that many leading financiers were actually Tories, nor that many Tories dabbled in finance: a convenient stereotype had evolved which was to influence the politics of the next half-century (**68, 91, 102**).

Banking and party politics

Indeed, the politics of finance were beginning to take priority over its techniques. Under the experienced Lord Treasurer Godolphin (1702–10) and his novice successor, Robert Harley (1710–14), the management of Queen Anne's finances during the War of the Spanish Succession was characterised less by innovation than by consolidation of, and improvement upon, the lessons of the 1690s (**70, 72**). Long-term borrowing was organised with boldness and short-term borrowing was handled with skill. The Land Tax once again yielded the major share of revenue and the Bank of England once again provided crucial support – at least until 1710. But in this year the Bank incautiously tried to intervene in the political sphere. Some of its directors, anxious about deteriorating public confidence, warned the Queen against the dismissal of the ministers they trusted, Godolphin above all. Their impertinence rebounded: Godolphin was dismissed, the Bank was discredited and every Tory prejudice against 'the monied interest' seemingly vindicated (**94**).

Until this débâcle the Bank had been riding high. In 1707 it secured a twenty-one-year extension of its charter, increased its capital and raised its dividends. In 1709 it doubled its capital, again raised its dividends and went on to underwrite the Treasury's plan 'to make all the Exchequer Bills as good as Money' (**53**, pp. 63–6). Now established as the principal source of short-term loans*, in 1710 it was entrusted for the first time with the agency for long-term loans. Its indispensability seemed assured (**72**, pp. 62, 360).

But the new Tory head of the Treasury, Robert Harley (soon Earl of Oxford), was prepared to prove otherwise. For some years now the Bank had been stalked by a vengeful chartered company which had started life respectably enough in 1691 as a genuine manufacturer of 'Hollow Sword Blades'. But by 1703 it had become a property and finance company, boldly trying to intrude upon the Bank's exclusive sphere by taking over government debt and attempting to underbid the Bank in offers for loans. It had failed, but in 1711 its directors were quickly at hand with a breathtaking scheme – to take over no less than £9 million of floating*, short-term government debt in return for incorporation* as 'the Governor and Company of Merchants of Great Britain trading to the South Seas' (**47**). This inspired opportunism was linked to the current peace negotiations with France and Spain from which England hoped to obtain valuable slave-trading privileges with the Spanish Americas – 'the South Seas'. Harley's patronage ensured the new company's launch, and it duly emerged to Tory cheers as a potential rival to the Bank of England as well as to the East India Company (which had been re-united in 1709) (**110**).

However, as a finance company the South Sea corporation soon proved a disappointment and as a trading company it was a virtual sham. The '*asiento*', or contract, for trade with South America was undermined by Spanish ill-will and English incompetence; the company's share-price sagged, and the Tory government soon realised that it still stood in need of the Bank's support. It was thus the Bank which handled the bulk of long-term borrowing*, while the South Sea Company sank momentarily into the background. Nevertheless, through Harley, it had already achieved something important. It had not merely relieved the public purse of £9 million of expensive floating debt: it had helped to resolve Defoe's conundrum, whether 'they that have the money must have the management' or 'they that have the management will have the money'. The latter now seemed more probable than it had before 1710. The myth of an omnipotent Whig 'monied interest' had been exploded – and so too was the myth of rustic Tory innocence.

5 Assessment, 1685–1714

Surveying the quarter-century since the 'Glorious Revolution', one cannot fail to be impressed by the remarkable fertility of the 1690s. The adoption of long-term borrowing, the foundation of a great bank, the recoinage of the metallic currency and the circulation of a paper one – any one of these would make their decade significant in financial history: together they unquestionably add up to a revolution. But it was a revolution with more than merely financial implications. The achievement was inseparable from a constitutional revolution which had placed parliamentary control of the purse at the heart of political power. That, as we have seen, had been a deliberate, non-partisan objective in the Commons of 1689–90, although its promoters cannot have foreseen all its consequences. The chief of these, though easily overlooked, was the principle of 'annuality' – that is, that every year the financial needs of government would have to be presented to Parliament by the ministers of the crown as estimates which would be submitted to careful scrutiny before being matched by adequate 'supply'. Estimates debates and Supply debates thus became central episodes in the parliamentary calendar, as they still are, and to these were soon added their logical sequel – the reports of parliamentary audit (**76**). From 1690 to 1697 and from 1702 to 1713 Commissions of Accounts headed by MPs sat in inquisition upon government expenditure, seeking and finding ample evidence of waste and corruption.

The experience was a formative one on the character of English politics for it helped in the development of a 'country' ideology and, it is argued, of a 'country party' which, cutting across Whig/Tory affiliations, is one of the most controversial themes in the historiography of the period (**71**, **91**, **102**). This 'country' ideology was closely linked to the generalised hostility against 'the monied interest' which has already been described, but it added to this a comprehensive resentment of government employees or 'placemen' whom it believed to have now grown so numerous as to distort the constitutional balance. Particularly feared was the growing army of revenue officials whose influence as the servants of the crown, in the constituencies and inside the Commons, ran counter to the ideal of parliamentary independence. They were consequently the principal target of a series of 'Place Bills' designed to oust them and other officeholders from the House, and although attempts at a total exclusion failed on four occasions between 1692 and 1700, the eviction of Commissioners of Customs and Commissioners of Excise together with other targeted officials was successfully provided for during William's reign. Under Anne the principle was extended in a form which was to take effect on her death and to govern membership of Parliament until the twentieth century: *all* MPs accepting offices 'or places of profit under the crown' were obliged to resign their seats (though they might seek re-election) and the total of such 'placemen' in the Commons was limited to the number already in existence (**36**, **100**, **102**).

Flanking this restraint on the influence of the executive were two other important constitutional measures – the Triennial Act of 1694, providing not merely for frequent parliaments but for short ones – and the Property Qualification Act of 1711, which sought to restrict membership of the Commons to independent country gentlemen with an adequate income from land. Both these measures, though comparatively shortlived or ineffectual, were carefully calculated attempts to offset the social and political consequences of the financial revolution; the former by neutralising corrupt influences, the latter by excluding 'the monied interest'.

These bitterly contested measures were the necessary price which the executive had to pay to the legislature for its greatly increased financial resources. But it was a price worth paying for what amounted to an administrative revolution, one measure of which is the considerable growth of England's administrative machinery (**43**, **102**, **155**). Small and weak by European standards in the early seventeenth century, it had been strenuously exercised by the wars against France and by 1714 had gained an unprecedented accretion of muscular power with its numbers of permanent employees probably quadrupled since the 1630s and tripled since the 1660s. This growth was visible not merely in the military departments (Army, Navy, Ordnance, Victualling, Sick and Wounded) but in the civil departments, such as the joint Secretaryships of State, the Board of Trade and – above all – the Treasury. Although comparatively small itself, with barely a dozen permanent clerks and senior officials, the Treasury presided over the largest administrative empire yet seen in English government (**173**). It gave orders to the Exchequer, with its 120 officials, and directed the proceedings of the numerous revenue-collecting agencies which had sprung up since 1688. For, joined to the Commissioners of Customs (1671) and the Commissioners of Excise (1683) were the Commissioners of Stamps (1694), the Commissioners of Hackney Coaches (1694), the Commissioners of Hawkers & Pedlars (1697), the Commissioners of Salt (1701) as well as other agencies, altogether employing some 6,000 officials. They represented an alarming concentration of patronage power which ensured that whoever ran the Treasury had claims to run the country.

But who ran the Treasury? The question has been often asked, even in this century. For, standing behind the Treasury Lords was the Secretaryship which, ever since the appointment of Sir George Downing (1667–71), had been held by some extraordinarily able men such as Henry Guy (1680–94) and William Lowndes (1694–1724). As confidential advisers, but also as independent Members of Parliament, they were curiously hybrid creatures performing a role which, in modern terms, was both that of senior civil servant and junior minister (**43**). They ran the department, directed the clerks, organised the business; but at the same time conceived, drafted and carried through Parliament much of the key financial legislation of their day. Downing's parliamentary activity was prodigious (**177**) as was that of Lowndes, who for thirty years masterminded the technical framework of the financial revolution.

Yet they did not lack for advice. Treasury files and state papers of the period still brim with the unsolicited financial schemes which flooded in from every quarter – some far-sighted (Sir Christopher Wren outlined a plan for decimal coinage in 1695) but some frankly lunatic. The presses too poured out a remarkable torrent of advice and criticism, much of which reflects the intense political passions of the time. On the whole, the Tories had the better of it, served as they were by some of the ablest writers of the day including Swift, Defoe and Davenant. Orchestrated by Robert Harley they were responsible for memorable indictments of the financial revolution (**75**). Davenant, in his *True Picture of a Modern Whig* of 1701, created 'Tom Double', the satirical epitome of a contemporary 'yuppie' whose cheating, intriguing, stock-jobbing career had brought him £50,000 – 'and 14 years ago I had not shoes to my feet'. Defoe, in his *Villainy of Stock-Jobbers Detected*, also of 1701, flayed the same class of men, and Swift in *The Conduct of the Allies* and *The History of the Four Last Years of Queen Anne's Reign* was to call down anathema upon 'the pernicious Counsels of borrowing Money upon publick Funds of Interest'.

Yet there is an interesting ambivalence detectable in these writers which suggests just how far they too had been captivated by the novelty and excitement of the financial revolution. Charles Davenant (1656–1714), an experienced Excise official, wrote invaluable treatises on taxation, borrowing and trade (**6**, **195**) which, while sharply critical, warmly embraced the financial achievements of the revolutionary decades. He rhapsodised on paper credit – 'this nerval juice', 'this huge engine of credit' – and exulted in the financial power which had out-fought France. Defoe likewise paid his patriotic tribute in essays of 1710, *Upon Public Credit* and *Upon Loans*, and even the irreconcilable Swift did not disdain to dabble in the money-market, buying Bank-stock for the rise in 1711. He was in a select but growing company. Dr P. G. M. Dickson, who analysed the investing community at several points, estimates that there were some 10 to 11,000 public creditors in 1709 of whom about 2,000 owned stock in the Bank of England (**72**, pp. 260–2). He found it to be a metropolitan clientele, with barely 15 per cent coming from the provinces, and also a cosmopolitan one with significant French, Dutch and Jewish investors, not all of whom were refugees. The major investors were drawn, almost inevitably, from the merchant class – plutocrats such as Sir James Bateman, Sir John Houblon and Sir Theodore Janssen (who were all at some time directors of the Bank of England) but there were also less ostentatious figures of the kind analysed by Dr D. W. Jones – solid men of business who showed a marked preference for stock in the Bank and the united East India Company (**117**, **118**). These merchants were, almost by definition, professional investors who looked for an ideal combination of security, high return and liquidity*. Not for them the long-term annuities, the unpredictable lotteries nor – if they could avoid them – the encumbrance of government 'tallies' assigned as payment for goods. 'Navy bills' – literally the unpaid bills of that department ranged in numerical sequence for payment in course – were a particularly risky commodity, for although they earned interest and were readily assignable* they carried no guarantee of early redemption* and were thus exchanged at a substantial discount*. Only the very wealthy could afford that degree of uncertainty and the rich rewards that came in time.

Thus, from early in its history the stock market offered a range of securities* – long-term, short-term, high-risk, low-risk – for income or for capital growth. The fruits of this financial revolution were inevitably distributed in rather unequal shares: to London's 'monied interest' of wealthy merchants and tradesmen in abundance, and to peers, gentry, government officials, professional men and rich widows in proportions which seem to differ little from those of Backwell's or Vyner's clientele in the 1660s. The mass of the population remained remote from these opportunities and the lives of even the 'middling sort', with family incomes of £30 to £150 p.a. (**101**), were touched at only a few points – by a Bank of England note, by a small Exchequer annuity or, most probably, by a gamble in a £10 lottery ticket split into 20 shares. The government lotteries of 1711–14 created 520,000 tickets at £10 and 38,000 at £100, and the prize drawings at the Guildhall or the Banqueting House, Whitehall, were great public occasions, attracting thousands and spread over many days (**80**). Successful for the Treasury, they were seductive for the public and they fed that speculative, gambling appetite which was soon to produce the most notorious episode in England's financial history.

Part Three: 1714–1760

6 The Fall and Rise of the London Money Market

The National Debt in 1714

Marlborough's victories and the 'War of the Spanish Succession' (1701–13) had added £35 million to England's debts and when George of Hanover succeeded to the throne in 1714 his government faced a mixture of liabilities totalling about £48 million – some old, some new and all costly.

1   Oldest of all was the legacy of Charles II, the Bankers' Debt dating from 1672. Standing at nearly £1.33 million in 1705, it had (after prolonged litigation) been finally acknowledged by the courts and by Parliament as an obligation of the state, but in view of the notorious fact that its ownership had passed to speculators at an average discount* of 50 per cent Parliament declined to authorise more than 3% p.a. interest upon the annuities – which amounted to the same as halving the capital sum at the standard rate of 6% p.a.

2   Next in seniority were the legacies of the 1690s, the high-interest-bearing long-term annuities known as 'irredeemables' which could not be legally extinguished before 1792–1807. They represented a debt of nearly £10 million at 7%, and some shorter annuities, expiring in the 1740s, amounted to a debt of some £2.5 million at 9%.

3   Then there were the annuities recently created by the lotteries of 1711–14, representing a capital obligation of £11.7 million which at least had the merit of being redeemable within thirty-two years.

4   To these must be added the state's obligations to the three great corporations'– £3.37 to the Bank of England, £3.2 million to the East India Company and the £9.2 million absorbed by the South Sea Company.

Altogether a 'national debt' totalling £40.3 million was 'funded' in the sense that Parliament had pledged public funds to the payment of interest (and, eventually, the capital) at rates ranging between 6 and 9% p.a. But to this must be added the unfunded debts, such as Exchequer Bills* worth about £4.5 million plus an indeterminate 'floating debt'* owed by the Navy, Ordnance and Victualling departments totalling perhaps £3 million more (**72**, p. 80).

All this posed a complex challenge to a peace-time government which could no longer rely on heavy taxation as a political option. The total interest burden, of £3 million p.a., was eating up half the government's reduced revenues, although interest rates in the private sector had fallen to 5% or less. Clearly something had to be done to convert the high-interest debts to lower rates and – if possible – pay off some of the debts. But how?

A combination of gentle arm-twisting and sugared bribes offered a partial solution. Individual creditors with redeemable annuities could be threatened with premature repayment unless they accepted a reduction of interest, and the great corporations might be 'persuaded' that it would be in their long-term interest to accept a little less. Legislation along these lines in 1717 succeeded in converting these selected liabilities to a rate of 5% p.a., thus saving nearly £326,000 p.a. which was to be set aside to buy up and cancel other debts. These savings were known as 'the Sinking Fund'* and in due course the operations of 1717 were to generate a fund worth over £1 million p.a. (**72**, p. 87).

But what could be done about the 'irredeemables'? Only a very compelling inducement would persuade owners of a safe, substantial and very nearly perpetual income to exchange it for something less substantial. This was the problem which the Treasury was pondering in 1716; it was still brooding on it in 1719.

John Law's 'System'

Fortunately, perhaps, England's dilemma was not unique. Decades of war had cost France very dear and on Louis XIV's death in 1715 her debts were equivalent to about £230 million. Awash with paper obligations, verging on bankruptcy, she too required drastic measures to convert high interest rates and redeem huge debts. A financial wizard was required – and miraculously he appeared in the person of John Law, a young Scottish banker on the run from a homicide charge. This remarkably resourceful and inventive man succeeded in making himself acceptable in French financial circles and by 1716 he had gained the ear of the French government. His 'scheme', unfolded in stages between 1716 and 1720, offered a daring combination of commercial exploitation, currency manipulation and large-scale debt redemption*. Basing its commercial credit on trading rights in French Louisiana, the 'Mississipi Company' of 1717 was closely linked to Law's Banque Générale which he had set up in 1716 but, like the English Sword Blade Company and the South Sea Company, the marriage of commercial potential with liquid capital was directed towards ambitious bids for larger and larger chunks of government debt upon which shareholders, dazzled by the Mississipi Company's prospects, were willing to accept lower and lower rates of interest. Success bred success. By mid-1719 Law was in control of the French Mint; by December he was virtually Minister for Finance, uniquely placed to inflate the value of his company's shares by immense issues of notes and successive flotations of stock. By 1720, amid mounting public hysteria, the share price of the Mississipi Company had risen tenfold (**47**, **145**).

This brilliant display of financial virtuosity did not go unnoticed in England. Alert investors started to transfer their funds from London and some speculators borrowed heavily to participate in the boom. By May 1720 it was estimated that £5 million had left England for French securities, which – if true – gives some idea of the volume of 'hot money' available in London. It was soon to find its domestic opportunity.

The South Sea 'Scheme'

Determined to match the French achievement, the directors of the South Sea Company offered their 'scheme' late in 1719. It envisaged nothing less than the incorporation of the entire English National Debt into the capital of their company. Holders of redeemable *and* irredeemable debt would, in effect, be bought out or bribed into becoming shareholders, voluntarily surrendering their fixed annuities for the less certain prospects of company dividends. Furthermore, the company would pay the Treasury for the privilege – offering over £3 million at first, and then more as the Bank of England tried to intervene with a rival bid. By February 1720, with the help of massive bribes, the South Sea Company had won the auction with a bid of £7.5 million and by April the scheme had been given parliamentary sanction in an elaborate measure (6 Geo. I, c. 4) drafted by William Lowndes.

It is easy to see what the state stood to gain. It would be

relieved, at a stroke, of a gigantic burden; the redeemables and the irredeemables with a capital valuation of £31 million would dissolve, voluntarily and without breach of public faith, into a private liability. True, the state would still have to pay the Company an assured interest of 5% p.a., falling to 4% after seven years, but this represented a considerable saving to the public purse in addition to the dowry of £7.5 million. It was nothing less than the 'privatisation' of the National Debt.

But it is less easy to understand what the South Sea Company or its potential shareholders stood to gain, for this was hypothetical. It rested on the possibility that the Company might be profitable and that its share price might rise, coupled with the certainty that for every £100 of debt taken over the Company could issue shares of an equivalent amount. Thus, potentially, if all the redeemable and irredeemables were subscribed, the Company could create £31 million of stock. But suppose the Company's shares did rise – say, double in value overnight? A £100 share, now worth £200, would cancel £200 of debt; £15.5 million-worth of stock would therefore clear the whole National Debt, leaving the Company free to sell as it pleased the remaining £15.5 million of stock which it was entitled to create.

In the event the shares did not double – they tripled in value. On 14 April, within a fortnight of the scheme's launch and before any debts were taken over, the Company was able to presume upon its virtual licence to print money by starting to sell £2.25 million of its anticipated surplus of stock at a price of 300 per cent [**doc. 15**]. A fortnight later it sold £1.5 million more at 400 per cent and seven weeks after that £5 million at 1000 per cent (that is, for £50 million). After ten more feverish weeks, on 24 August, a fourth issue of £1.25 million was made at 1,000 per cent amid scenes of frenzied public demand (**72**, p. 124). The South Sea Company directors had successfully recreated in 'Change Alley the kind of Gadarene stampede which had been witnessed in Paris and each subscription of stock was filled within hours. Carried along with this mass excitement the owners of irredeemable annuities could no longer resist. Eighty per cent of their assets were eagerly surrendered for the Company's stock, as were 85 per cent of the redeemables. By the end of operations £26 million of the public's claims on the National Debt had been handed over for South Sea Company shares with a face value of £10 million, though in fact subscribers only received £8.5 million, leaving the Company free to dispose of £17.5 million on the open market at vastly inflated prices (**72**, p. 136).

The Bubble

How was it done, and why? What possessed the owners of sound annuities and even sounder money to part with their assets for the chimaera of South Sea stock? The Company's trading prospects were dim, its real assets were meagre and the government's proposed annuity of 5%, later 4%, made a poor exchange for the existing guarantee of 6 to 9%.

The conventional answer tends to be a moralising one which stresses the timeless propensity of human avarice to feed upon rumour and illusion, particularly when manipulated by unscrupulous schemers. These ingredients were certainly all present in 1720. The greed for instant gain was almost palpable in the mobs which besieged 'Change Alley at every issue of stock, and the South Sea Company directors played upon the public with every trick of promotional publicity. They fed the midsummer madness with a bogus dividend; they placed huge quantities of unbought stock with friends, ministers and Members of Parliament; they re-lent the share-proceeds to assist fresh purchases and massaged the price to its peak in July. Deceptively little was required of investors. To subscribe for shares at 400, for example, a down-payment of only £40 was required: the balance was payable in nine instalments over the next three years. But, once possessed of his 'scrip' (that is, the receipt-note for a subscription), the investor could immediately enter the market and sell (or buy more) as the price soared towards 1,000. Who could resist? Hundreds of men and women, the rich and not-so-rich, were drawn in by hope, by greed and even by fashion. 'The town is quite mad about the South Sea,' someone wrote; 'it is being very unfashionable not to be in the South Sea' (**116**, **145**).

This gambling mania soon spread beyond the orbit of the South Sea Company. A wave of speculative projects more numerous than those of the 1690s swept through London, filling the press with their spurious claims. As *Mist's Journal* (a weekly paper) reported on 11 June:

> This week there has been a great Stroke in the Alley; a Multitude of new Bubbles, Projects, subscriptions, etc, have been set a foot, and every single one has been publicly advertised to exceed the rest. The several sums proposed to be raised in this Manner, amount to since Saturday last about 224,000,000 pound Sterling (**148**, p. 51).

The investing mania swept on, to Amsterdam, to Hamburg and

beyond. Funds came back from France, where Law's 'scheme' was beginning to subside. Altogether an estimated 30,000 people may have been drawn into the South Sea Company's 'scheme' alone, representing (Dr Dickson suggests) three-quarters of the entire investing public in England (**72**, pp. 161, 272–3). Not all were innocent victims and few were poor. Many peers and half of the House of Commons acquired stock, as did civil servants, lawyers and clergy. And not all of them were to lose their shirts. Sir Isaac Newton doubled his money and the philanthropic book-seller Thomas Guy, who sold out in time, cleared a fortune which helped towards the foundation of his great hospital. But those who did lose – the great majority – composed a terrifying, vengeful and influential army whose demand for compensation and reform was to shape the future course of the financial revolution.

The Bubble bursts

The collapse of the South Sea Company's share price was almost inevitable once investors woke up to the hollowness of its commercial prospects. But they were remarkably slow to do so, and it took the conjunction of several external influences to divest them of their illusions. The advance of plague in western Europe and violent industrial disorders at home contributed to an undercurrent of uncertainty, and there was serious unease at the scale of unscrupulous company promotions. Legislation against unauthorised corporations was rushed through Parliament and emerged as the so-called 'Bubble Act' of June 1720 (**77**). It was not this, however, which checked the boom in share prices, which had yet to reach their peak: it was, rather, the Treasury's decision in August (supported by the South Sea Company's own directors) to take action against rival enterprises which eventually burst the bubble. Thus, although the fourth flotation of shares at 1,000 was fully subscribed within three hours on 24 August, the share price soon began to fall. It had reached 775 on 1 September, 520 on the 16th and by 1 October stood at only 290. Bank of England and East India Company stocks followed a similar trajectory and long before Parliament reassembled in December it was clear that England faced an unprecedented financial catastrophe (**72**, p. 139).

The effect of the share-collapse was to leave thousands of investors in a serious plight, although they were not all in quite the same boat. First there were the 'money subscribers' who had paid up their initial instalment for over-priced stock and who now stood committed to paying off the remainder. Some had borrowed from the Company to finance their subscription* and were thus doubly in its debt, with no remaining prospect of capital gain and little of future dividends. They perhaps were least to be pitied, for their 'losses' were essentially a mirage of the huge gains they had expected to make in an ever-rising market. Thus the Duke of Chandos (who as plain James Brydges had made £600,000 as Paymaster of the Forces between 1707 and 1712) bewailed his 'loss' of a further £580,000 between August and September, but it was a paper loss which still left him seriously rich, as were many other bleating victims.

The real losers were the annuitants – those owners of irredeemable and redeemable government securities who had voluntarily surrendered them for South Sea Company stock. By the time of the crash they had got little in return and it seemed possible that they would get little in the future. They had no remaining claim on the government's purse, and any claims they might feel they had on its conscience were prejudiced by certain ministers' deep implication in the Company's frauds. Among them were the Chancellor of the Exchequer, John Aislabie, a Secretary of State, James Craggs and his father, the Joint Postmaster General, James Craggs senior.

The investing public's consequent rage and despair was thus directed at two guilty parties – the directors of the South Sea Company and their highly placed friends in the government. Both were duly dealt with after lengthy parliamentary investigation – by dismissal, imprisonment and the confiscation of their estates (**116, 145**). Some took refuge in flight, others in suicide. A fatal seizure carried off Lord Stanhope, the senior Secretary of State, and in April 1721 the prime minister, the Earl of Sunderland, announced his resignation. The most immediate effect of the South Sea débâcle was thus the emergence of Robert Walpole as First Lord of the Treasury, a position he was to retain for the next twenty-one years (**154**).

Sir Robert Walpole

At forty-four years of age, Robert Walpole was already an experienced financial administrator. It was he who had handled the conversion of government stocks to 5% and inaugurated the Sinking Fund* in 1717. But he now faced an infinitely more complex problem, whose intricate solution defies any simple summary. Essentially, his achievement was to recapture public confidence in the integrity of the government's financial dealings and to preserve the central objective of the South Sea Company's scheme – namely, the conversion* of a large portion of long-term, fixed-interest National Debt into a redeemable, low-interest stock. This meant that the unfortunate annuitants would have to live with their mistake, receiving annuities from the South Sea Company which were worth only between one-third and two-thirds as much as those they had enjoyed from the Exchequer. The money subscribers too would have to accept a greatly curtailed investment and count themselves lucky that they had escaped from their full obligation to repay loans and complete their subscriptions. The South Sea Company's inflated debts were rescheduled (with the help of its old enemy, the Bank of England) and its capital written down and then split in two, one half representing the trading capital with which the Company made feeble and ultimately futile attempts to carry on business with South America. It ceased trading in 1750. The other half became, like the Bankers' Debt, a permanent liability on which the Exchequer paid a modest interest until 1850, when Gladstone redeemed the capital and the Company finally disappeared (**185**).

The story of the South Sea Bubble has been often told in modern times, vividly by John Carswell (**47**) and analytically by P. G. M. Dickson (**72**, pp. 90–156). It has every claim to be regarded as the 'grand climacteric' of the financial revolution, for it marks both the height and the depth to which the ingenuity and stupidity, the imagination and credulity of its participants could attain. Tainted though it was by fraud, incompetence and unbridled greed it nonetheless exhibits remarkable features of financial daring and virtuosity. But it was certainly not an exclusively English phenomenon. The events in London were echoed in several other western capitals, and they can be regarded as the deferred price paid in common by Europe for the costly struggles with Louis XIV (**25**). Years of extraordinary financial exertion had created a dangerous imbalance within the major economies by placing higher premiums on money-market speculation than on trading, manufacturing or agricultural investment, and neither government nor society had sufficient experience to avert the consequences. Thus, with hindsight, the catastrophe of 1720 could be viewed as a salutary lesson. In England it certainly ensured that future governments would stand or fall by their financial competence. Sound budgeting and the skilful courtship of the money market henceforth became an essential political art, of which Walpole demonstrated himself to be the master.

For contemporaries the lesson seemed less benign. The 'Bubble' was variously viewed, in apocalyptic terms, either as a madness, or a disease, or a divinely ordained retribution. Fuel for a thousand sermons and innumerable satirical gibes, it was clearly a traumatic experience which could not be comfortably assimilated within the normal patterns of human affairs. Indeed, although the events of 1720 hardly rank in horror or mortality with the plague of 1665, it has been argued that Defoe conflated the two disasters and that his *Journal of the Plague Year*, published in 1722, was both an historical reconstruction of the 1660s and a pointed allegory of 1720 (**170**). Be that as it may, the Bubble evidently left a deep mark on English consciousness which is discernible in the writings not only of Defoe but of Swift and Pope, as well as in the savage pessimism of Hogarth's satirical prints [**doc. 16**].

7 After the Crash

The political consequences were profound enough and might have been worse if the Jacobites and the Pretender had exploited the crisis, but in the event the emergence of Walpole as undisputed 'premier minister' ushered in a long period of financial consolidation and comparative stability. Indeed, although the forty years after 1720 were to produce two major wars and a Jacobite invasion, with all their attendant financial stress, the main interest of the financial revolution after the Bubble lies much less in its response to crises than in its shaping of normality.

For the institutions which embody the revolution – the funded debt, the Bank of England, the stock market and all their attendant products – now ceased to be seen as precarious novelties designed for emergencies and became acceptable features of normal life with important roles to play. True, the National Debt continued to be regarded in some quarters as an insupportable and corrupting burden, but for increasing numbers of people government securities were to occupy an indispensable place at the foundation of personal as well as national credit. Once the shock of the Bubble and its consequences had been overcome the structure of 'the Funds' became an object of pride, widely envied abroad and keenly supported at home at every new issue of government stock. By the 1750s government loans were invariably over-subscribed and the consequent securities often sold at above par*. 'Consols'* now came of age as the centre-piece of a remarkably stable system of public credit.

This achievement was largely the work of Sir Robert Walpole between 1721 and 1742, and of his successor as First Lord of the Treasury *and* Chancellor of the Exchequer, Henry Pelham (1743–54). If their paramount objective as statesmen was to reduce the burden of taxation (and particularly the Land Tax), their second – which was a necessary precondition of the first – was the containment of the National Debt. This policy required the reduction of its capital and of its interest but necessarily fell short of its total abolition, which would have been as undesirable as it was improbable.

61

For it was now plausible to argue that the existence of 'the Funds' and all the accompanying machinery for their registration, transfer and payment of dividends, constituted a national resource which enabled the government to meet national crises when they came. As it was, containment was demanding enough and called for skilful management through the selective substitution of expensive old debts with cheaper new ones. Thus, Walpole floated a series of new loans totalling £6.5 million, mostly at 4% and 3% and, with the help of the Sinking Fund*, repaid £12.8 million of old liabilities bearing 5% or more (**72**, p. 210). This meant that, although the capital of the Debt had been reduced by barely 10 per cent, its annual interest charges had fallen by a fifth. Pelham pursued a similar strategy, although driven off course by the War of the Austrian Succession (1744–48). This cost England over £95 million, of which nearly one-third was added to the National Debt. By 1749 Pelham faced a total debt of £70 million, of which £57.7 million was at 4%, the rest at 3%. His solution was a bold one, warmly applauded by a landowning Parliament though received with hostility by the City. In November 1749 he proposed that the 4% stocks should be speedily reduced to 3.5% and then, after seven years, to only 3%. The owners of such stocks had until February 1750 to decide to accept (**189**).

Pelham's conversion*

Reactions to Pelham's scheme demonstrate just how deeply and widely the investing public was now involved in government securities. Dr Dickson has estimated that there were between 50,000 and 60,000 government creditors in the 1750s (**72**, pp. 284–5) with ownership still heavily skewed towards a plutocracy of powerful financiers and corporations. Their collaboration was essential to the success of Pelham's proposals (which meant, after all, a 25 per cent reduction in their dividends) and it was not immediately forthcoming. But the chain of reasoning which eventually won their assent was compelling: the general tendency of interest rates was downwards, and if they rejected returns of 3.5% and 3% from the Treasury they would be lucky to get more elsewhere, on worse security. Indeed, security was the key. Despite the discredit of the Bubble – or rather, because of it – government stock now had unimpeachable reliability. It was efficiently administered, faithfully redeemed and eagerly sought after. It increasingly changed hands at, or occasionally above, its face value. Already, as Pelham spoke, the 3% stocks were selling at par.* Thus, to offset their loss of interest, holders of the older stocks could reasonably look forward to some capital appreciation as their 4% holdings, bought perhaps when they stood at as little as 70 or 80, rose to be worth 100 or more at 3%.

Eventually Pelham secured the voluntary surrender of 88 per cent of all the 4% stocks, and the Treasury was able to mop up the residue easily enough. Further tidying operations followed as the medley of old loans bearing 3% were consolidated into one large stock, centrally administered through the Bank of England. It was thus that 'consols' were born, the premier gilt-edged stock of the English Funds which by December 1752 was selling for 106⅜, a price not to be equalled before the high noon of Victorian prosperity (**72**, p. 243).

Pelham's conversion and consolidation operations of mid-century conveniently mark the zenith of the financial revolution. They were a triumph for government debt management and rounded off the complex legacies of the 1690s and Marlborough's wars. They also laid a sound foundation for the trials which lay ahead in the huge expenditures of the Seven Years War and the War of American Independence, when loans of undreamed-of size were to be sought and found with comparative ease.

The financial Establishment

Yet the achievements of Walpole and Pelham were not won single-handed, and their significance was not confined to the public sector. They were built upon the ingenuity and co-operation of a wider community of advisers and financiers and their implications affected the economy as a whole.

Among the advisers the role of Treasury officials can be all too easily overlooked, for it remained a small department whose permanent officials were often idle (**173**). But in its 'Revenue Room' and among its Chief Clerks and, above all, in its Joint Secretaries, the Treasury sometimes possessed outstanding financial experts. The great William Lowndes, a Treasury clerk since 1675 and Joint Secretary between 1694 and 1724, has already been cited for his unique contribution to the formative years of the financial revolution. He was succeeded by the no less remarkable John Scrope who died in harness in 1752, aged ninety, after guiding Walpole and Pelham through their most difficult years. Through Secretaries such as James West, Samuel Martin and Charles Jenkinson this tradition of expert knowledge was passed on to the days of the Younger Pitt and beyond.

But, crucial to the Treasury's work was an intimate acquaintance with 'the City' and its leaders. As early as 1710 it had been recognised that the Treasury required first-hand knowledge of the stock and commodity markets and it was recommended that a senior official should haunt the Royal Exchange to seek out 'the opinions of the ablest and most knowing persons in the City' (**174**, pp. 174–5). Formally and informally, through letters, interviews, personal knowledge and confidential closeting, the Treasury's contacts were maintained with the directorates of the Bank, the great trading companies and other leaders of 'the monied interest'. Collaboration with this financial 'Establishment' became highly systematised in the decades following the Bubble.

The Bank of England had emerged from that crisis with its reputation slightly tarnished, for – like others with lesser responsibilities – it had been carried away by the South Sea mania and was not wholly unscathed. However, its superior credit not only carried it through the crisis but enabled it to prop up Walpole's complex settlement of the South Sea Company's affairs, and thereafter its relations with the government have been described as 'smooth and easy' (**53**, p. 91). They were certainly lucrative. Its capital, increased to £9.8 million by 1742, yielded annual dividends of 6 or 5% between 1721 and 1758. With its charter extended in 1713 and 1742, its role as banker to the state was placed beyond doubt and gave a foundation of stability to the money market as a whole. Its note issue, re-designed and better printed after 1725 in standard denominations (**93**, p. 27), circulated widely and its underwriting of Exchequer bills assured the government of a reliable float of ready cash. Handling the registration and transfer paperwork for 70 per cent of government stocks by 1760, the bookkeeping functions of the Bank (which had moved into Threadneedle Street in 1734) were a mundane but important service to the thousands of stock-holders who now looked to the Bank, not the Exchequer, for their regular payments of dividends [**doc. 19**].

Yet, although the Bank monopolised note-issue and much else, it did not monopolise wealth, and the Treasury was obliged to look further afield for those long-term loans it sometimes needed. It looked with increasing frequency to a comparatively small coterie in the City which could be counted upon to underwrite any loan – if suitably rewarded. Terms would be mutually agreed and confidential lists of prospective subscribers drawn up which bound the lead-managers in honour, if not in law, to pay up when called. They invariably did pay, for they had much to gain. A 'call' *only required them to find the first of several instalments. Once they possessed their 'scrip'* they were free to sell, and since government loans were invariably floated at an official discount* but soon commanded a premium* in the open market the initial subscribers stood to make handsome capital gains. For example, Henry Fox (Sir Stephen's son) put his name down for £300,000 in the £12 million loan of 1761 issued at a 20 per cent discount and, after increasing his and his associates' investment to nearly £774,000, sold out with a profit of about £103,000 (**187**, p. 430).

It was the scale of these privileged profits which generated a further back-lash against 'the monied interest'. Although no longer a Whig/Tory issue, the gulf between the profiteering 'ins' and the tax-paying 'outs' was still a wide and bitter one, and their conflict began to acquire some unpleasant racial and sectarian overtones. For on the one side stood prominent financiers like the Jewish-born Sampson Gideon (1699–1762), on the other the Quaker-born merchant, Sir John Barnard (1685–1764). Barnard, as Member of Parliament for the City of London, 1722–61, and its Lord Mayor in 1737–38, was an influential antagonist of stock-jobbers and politicians alike, whom he accused of collusion to rob the public. In 1737 he started an intensive economic debate by demanding massive reduction of the National Debt, both interest and principal, and in 1747 he successfully championed the case for 'open' subscriptions to government loans, as opposed to the prevailing system of closed, secret lists (**72**, p. 212–14). As a result the Treasury loans of 1747, for £5 million at 4%, were thrown open to the general public and were heavily oversubscribed with proffers of nearly £9 million. But in 1748 the 'open' subscription for £6 million began to falter. Gideon, whose private list of £600,000 in 1742 grew to over £1 million by 1746, came to the rescue in 1745 when the Jacobite invasion created a financial panic and he and his associates now came in to salvage the loan of 1748 (**189**).

Thereafter, throughout the Seven Years War and the War of American Independence, it was the 'closed' system of professionally negotiated subscriptions which usually prevailed, for while Barnard's ideas had some merit, the balance of practicality lay with those known as the 'Gideonites'. The Treasury could not afford the uncertainties of public subscriptions, and it too had something to gain, for in addition to the private lists headed by major financiers there were always important lists of ministers and Members of Parliament and – not least – 'the Treasury list' which included some of the department's prosperous and well-connected clerks who did very well out of the privilege. For better or worse, this aspect of the financial revolution had proved too important to be left to the amateurs.

Another of Barnard's campaigns against professional financial intermediaries also proved ineffectual. This culminated in his 1734 Act of Parliament 'to prevent the infamous Practice of Stock-Jobbing' (7 Geo. II, c. 8) and was designed to put an end to the speculative dealing in 'options' and 'bargains for time' which, since its earliest inception, had been a feature of the London stock market [**doc. 10**]. Essentially, the practices involved were gambles on the price of stocks at a future date and one's winnings did not necessarily depend on actual ownership of the stock. As Houghton had explained to his readers in 1694: for a small premium one could buy from a dealer either a 'put' – that is, the option to sell to him at a specified price, or a 'refusal' – the option to buy. Settlement between the parties was made at fixed intervals which, by the 1740s, had become quarterly. Then (for example), if one possessed a 'refusal' to take a specific amount of Bank stock at 150, but its market price had reached 160 on settlement day, one could exercise the option and either buy from the dealer at 150 cheerfully enough or, more cheerfully, receive from him the cash difference and leave the stock unbought. If, on the other hand, the stock had fallen to 140 one did not exercise the option and accepted the loss of the premium. But in either of the last two cases, neither party need ever actually own the gambled stock, although both had an interest in its vigorous fluctuation. Dealers who were gambling on a rise were known as 'Bulls' – probably because they sought to toss ever higher the price of their stock. Those who required a fall were 'Bears', perhaps (it is thought) because their plight was like that of the proverbial bear-skin seller who had not yet shot his bear (**72**, p. 503) Whatever the origin of these still familiar terms, both animals were thought to be dangerous. By rumour, innuendo, manipulation and sometimes fraud they were believed to distort the operations of the market and deceive the genuine investor. It was for this reason that they bore all the stigma which was conveyed by the eighteenth-century usage of the word 'jobber'.

Barnard's Act sought to cleanse the market of all this gambling and make it illegal to 'sell' stocks which were not actually owned [**doc. 17**]. But the borderline between the 'jobbers' and the 'brokers' who, if licensed, were perfectly legal, remained rather blurred and, although they were officially proscribed, stock-jobbers appear to have remained an important feature of the financial world, honouring verbal bargains which were unenforceable at law and making a market in all the stocks that offered (**60**). They were the professionals who dominated the teeming booths of Jonathan's coffee-house in 'Change Alley which had become, to all intents and purposes, the stock exchange, and theirs was the obscure jargon of 'Rescounters', 'Contangos', 'Bulls', 'Bears', 'Stags', 'Lame Ducks', 'Light Horse' and 'Heavy Horse', 'Omnium' and all the rest (**197**). Yet, despite this superficial obscurity, the stock market had acquired enough institutional maturity to make it comparatively attractive and accessible to the amateur investor. John Mortimer demonstrated this in 1761 when he published *Every Man his own Broker*. It ran through two editions in that year, and became a long-term best-seller. It was a compact celebration of the financial revolution, as well as a shrewdly satirical but informative guide to the market's complexities and its malpractices [**doc. 20**].

8   Assessment, 1714–1760

But how large and active was that market, and its clientele? Was it an efficient barometer of the wider economy, and did it in any way regulate its activities? Did it really serve the capital requirements of a country that was on the eve of its industrial revolution? And how did it rate upon the international stage of financial competition? These are some of the questions one must pose to assess the significance of England's financial revolution. Not all of them are answerable.

The investing public

Dr P. G. M. Dickson's painstaking analysis of the eighteenth-century investing public depicts a community which had grown steadily from about 10,000 in the reign of Queen Anne to some 60,000 at the accession of George III (a quantum leap to over 500,000 government creditors in 1815 lay ahead) (**72**, pp. 285–6). Setting aside the overseas component for the moment, the domestic element retained some consistent features. It was largely resident in London and the south-east of England, and the provincial element – over one-quarter in the 1690s – had diminished to below 10 per cent by the 1750s. Widows and spinsters, on the other hand, were a significant minority group which tended to grow, exhibiting a selective concentration on the safer stocks, such as South Sea annuities, Bank of England and East India Company shares. Though some of them were very wealthy indeed, women were not in general among the bigger investors. A well-to-do middle group of men owning £1,000 to £4,999, controlled 40 to 50 per cent of some stocks, and there was an increasingly powerful plutocracy with holdings in excess of £10,000 which controlled between a quarter and a third of the market, although numbering only 2 to 3 per cent of its investors. Among this tiny minority were the super-rich who gave the 'monied interest' its unpopular contemporary image, including as it did such patently alien names as Gideon, Salvador, Van Neck and Craisteyn. These men were often crucial to the successful flotation of the government's loans, although as long-term owners of stock they were perhaps less significant than a group of overseas investors and certain corporate participants in the market.

Insurance companies

Among the latter, perhaps the most interesting are the insurance companies, which were themselves an important by-product of the financial revolution. Marine insurance of shipping and cargoes had a longer history (**37**) but several house-insurance schemes had sprung up in post-Fire London or during the 'projecting' boom of the 1680s and 1690s. Among the promoters of new, corporate insurance companies were assiduous advocates of Land Banks, lotteries and other projects such as Nicholas Barbon and Thomas Neale, who epitomise the versatile, enterprising spirit of that time. Some of their legacies (such as Neale's 'Seven Dials Pillar', restored to central London in 1989) were to prove lasting. By the mid-eighteenth century there were more than a dozen insurance companies, some of which – the Sun (of 1710) and the Royal Exchange (of 1720) – are still thriving. Their investment policies were necessarily cautious and precluded both the more volatile and the least liquid securities, but by the 1750s the London Assurance and the Amicable Society were among the bigger corporate influences on the stock market (**114**, **141**). With them were institutions such as the Bank of England, the Court of Chancery and the agents of the Church of England, whose presence testifies conclusively to the established respectability and security of the eighteenth-century money market.

An efficient market?

It was also, by mid-century, a less hectically active market. The turnover in securities traded in 'Change Alley had tended to level out, although the services and machinery for buying and selling, registering and transferring stock ownership had much improved. Matching this relative decline in volume was an absolute decline in press coverage. Although the monthly *Gentleman's Magazine* (founded in 1731) carried a statistical record of share prices and exchange rates as a matter of course, the number of corporate stock quoted in Castaing's *Course of the Exchange* shrank to a mere handful of 'blue-chip'* stocks – the Bank of England, the East India Company, the South Sea Company, the Royal Exchange Assurance and a very few others – ignoring the scores of smaller incorporated companies that issued shares (**141**). This observation has raised questions about the technical efficiency of the London stock market. For example, did it really provide accurate means for translating information about economic conditions and business performance into the price of a corporate stock (as the financial markets are expected to do today)? Or were eighteenth-century investors naïve and sanguine creatures of habit, indifferent to the underlying merits or deficiencies of their business economy? Professor Mirowski's tentative answer to these questions is that the London stock market performed moderately well as a barometer of the real economy and that by the mid-eighteenth century it has the characteristics of an under-utilised, rather than an under-developed, market (**142**, p. 123).

Financial crises

Inevitably, that market sprang into bouts of frantic activity during national crises – which were invariably related to war or rumours of war – and when this happened the consequences might ripple quickly through financial networks well beyond the orbit of London. Starting with a fall in the price of government stocks and a rise in the market rate of interest (still limited by the usury laws to a maximum of 5%) there tended to follow a contraction of bank lending to private clients and a constraint on the availability of mortgages* (**35**, **115**). Business credit would feel the pinch; short-term loans might be called in and bankruptcies could follow. There could also be adverse movements in the rate of exchange. And, if the crisis was really acute, the Bank of England could be called into play as 'lender of last resort' – pacifying merchants by discounting their bills of exchange and relieving business anxieties by issuing bullion and cashing its notes on demand (**130**).

Any or all of these consequences have been traced at intervals up to the mid-eighteenth century, notably in 1701, 1710, 1715, 1720, 1726, and 1745, though their range and intensity varied from crisis to crisis (**35**). As Dr Julian Hoppit has found, the Jacobite invasion crises of 1715 and 1745 produced few bankruptcies (despite their alarming effect on the financial community) and the impact of the South Sea Bubble itself was less marked in terms of business failures than the trade depression of the late 1720s (**105**, **106**). Furthermore, the incidence of bankruptcy as a measure of financial crisis was always disproportionately higher in London, and the repercussions of crises in public finance tended to penetrate less deeply into the provincial economy of England than did those of trade-crises or bad harvests. Indeed, the wars of the period – which adversely affected the metropolitan money market and created tax burdens on the country at large – could give a selective stimulus to certain sectors of the provincial economy. They produced both prosperity and depression in an unpredictable mix (**106**, p. 128).

Provincial capital markets

These discrepancies between the behaviour of public and private finance, and between London and the provinces, supports the authoritative verdict that 'there was no *national* capital market in eighteenth-century England' (**133**, p. 92). For while it is true that the demands of government finance made huge incursions through taxation and borrowing, and that provincial businessmen relied heavily on London for credit and the settlement of bills of exchange, it is well established that there existed in provincial England semi-autonomous sources of capital and credit which were fully capable of meeting many local needs (**29–31**, **140**). Recent analysis of over 100,000 insurance policies (*c.* 1780) suggests the conclusion that wealth was less unevenly distributed between the English regions than has often been supposed (**113**). Furthermore, it is clear that, even before the rapid rise of 'country banking' in the late eighteenth century, local savings were being effectively channelled into local investment by country attorneys* who, like their scrivener* forebears, were well placed to identify local opportunities and draw up suitable securities* (**29**, **135, 140**). The mortgage was, of course, their principal product and as an investment vehicle its popularity with both lenders and borrowers grew throughout the century. At the same time, in areas such as Lancashire, research has revealed networks of local credit serving the needs of commerce, construction and small-scale manufacturing (**30**). Such networks appear to have been relatively immune to the attractions of the London money market and were left unmoved by the rise or fall of national stocks. They generally embodied the funds of widows and spinsters, executors and trustees and other passive investors whose demand for a secure, local, long-term investment often out-stripped the local supply (**97, 133**).

The London bankers

Even in London there was localised specialisation in financial services. The thirty or more private banks, which had grown out of the

71

goldsmith-shops of the late seventeenth century and had survived the crises of the early eighteenth century, were differentiated by their location, their clientele and their consequent investment policies. Thus, there were 'West-End' banks along Fleet Street and the Strand, such as Hoare's, or Child's, or Gosling's, which served an aristocratic and landed clientele and tended to specialise in mortgages, with only a discreet balance of investment in government stocks and mercantile credit (**120**). The banking philosophy of these modest partnerships (with assets much smaller than those of Charles II's bankers) is charmingly conveyed by a memorandum of 1746 [**doc. 18**].

Meanwhile, in Lombard Street there remained the 'City' banks with a mercantile clientele whose needs were more varied and demanding. Loans on the credit of trade goods, foreign bills of exchange and investment in the entire range of stock-market securities figure normally in their assets. These banks also had an important provincial dimension: they dealt with country-wide business clients, discounting their inland bills and channelling their balances into both the short-term and the long-term ends of the London money market. But it is significant that the late-eighteenth-century growth of this sector came from outside London, with the entry of provincial brewers, distillers, manufacturers and financiers into the London banking scene (**157**). The inference must be that, for all the sophistication of the mid-eighteenth-century financial system, provincial requirements were not being adequately served.

The Financial Revolution and the Industrial Revolution

This raises an awkward question, the answer to which properly belongs outside the scope of this survey but which is too important to ignore: what, if anything, did the financial revolution contribute to the genesis of the industrial revolution?

In so far as they have confronted the issue, economic historians have been reluctant to give an unequivocal verdict. Deeply divided about the primacy of 'demand' or 'supply' in generating industrial growth, unable to measure accurately the components of either and uncertain on which side to place the role of financial capital, they have either evaded the question entirely or have treated it with extreme diffidence (e.g. **63**, **69**, **82**, **143**). However, this reluctance has not been based upon a disregard for the money market and the importance of government finance. Quite the contrary. In one of the best discussions of the problem it has been pointed out that, while it cost about £1,000 million to defeat Revolutionary and Napoleonic France by 1815, the entire capital investment in canals by then was only £20 million and in the cotton industry about £10 million (**133**). The financial requirements of the early industrial revolution (it is argued) were thus too modest and too localised to register significantly upon national flows of investment. Conversely, while the indirect effects of metropolitan interest rates, discounts and credit supply impinged upon local investment decisions, they did not seriously impair industrial enterprise which could draw upon adequate local resources.

Thus, regarded from a provincial standpoint, the financial revolution of the early eighteenth century, with all its institutional offspring and its stable structure of securities, would seem to have made little contribution to early industrialisation: unless, of course, one poses a series of counterfactual questions. What would have happened to the society and economy of late-eighteenth-century England with an ill-managed National Debt, a discredited Bank of England, a defunct stock market, an inoperable fiscal system and the consequent probabilities of military defeat? Opinions on these hypothetical questions will differ, but it is difficult to discard the assumption that the development, if not the actual genesis, of the industrial revolution would have taken a less impressive course if it had not been able to call, directly or indirectly, upon the resources of a secure, versatile and prosperous financial sector. There appears to be much justice in the assertion that 'the most important economic development outside agriculture in the eighteenth century was the financial revolution based in London and centred upon the foundation of the Bank of England, the creation of the national debt, and the rise of the Stock Exchange' (**46**).

Foreign investment in England

A final, contemporaneous verdict on the financial revolution and its significance is provided by foreign investment in English stocks. By 1750 this was drawn from almost every quarter of Europe – from France, Germany, Switzerland, Italy, the Austrian empire and Russia – as well as from North America (**72**, p. 330). Above all, substantial investment was drawn from the Dutch, and it is this component which has attracted most attention, for it reflects the asset-preference of the most sophisticated investing community in the western world (**48**, **49**, **166**, **197**).

P. G. M. Dickson has estimated foreign holdings in major sectors of the National Debt as rising from just under 10 per cent in 1723–24 to just under 20 per cent by 1750 (**72**, p. 320). However, by the latter date foreign holdings in certain stocks were proportionately larger. In East India Company stock foreign holdings account for a quarter, and in Bank stock for a third – an order of magnitude which explains much contemporary unease at the vulnerability of England's financial system to foreign manipulation [**doc. 17**]. Overall, the foreign component in government securities by mid-century was nearly 15 per cent, and the Dutch proportion of this was over three-quarters.

The Dutch investment in England has a long history and much of it runs parallel with the financial revolution. Indeed, it seems so inseparable from it as to give plausibility to the revolution's alternative description as 'Dutch finance'. The connection arose naturally enough from intimate trading relations, favourable Dutch trade balances and, by the 1670s, from a mutual and increasing opposition to France. In 1669 it was alleged that there was as much as £200,000 of Dutch money on deposit in London (for which, it must be said, there is no evidence in surviving bankers' ledgers). However, it is evident that short-term trading balances were often held by English merchants on behalf of their Dutch correspondents and that these were sometimes reinvested in the English East India Company's bonds*. Even in 1672, at the height of another Anglo-Dutch war, Amsterdam merchants were shipping their cash reserves to trusted London agents to keep them out of the hands of the French (**178**, pp. 140, 181, 350). In due course, the union of Orange and Stuart and the revolution of 1688 were to consolidate a relationship which was never sentimental. Dutch investors were experienced as well as discerning and had long been accustomed to a structure of securities (mainly annuities) linked to long-term public borrowing which was proportionately greater than that of England. But their interest rates were usually lower and their taxes always higher, and the English National Debt offered them real premiums which explain the rapid growth of Dutch holdings after 1720. These were significant not merely for England but for the Dutch too – for in a century during which they lent large sums to every European country as well as the infant United States their investments in London remained much the largest.

Not surprisingly, therefore, close analysis of the short-term and long-term rates in the London and Amsterdam money markets from the 1730s onwards finds a growing convergence in their levels and fluctuations which argues for their increasing integration (**78**) – alas, just before the fourth Anglo-Dutch War of 1780–84 and the beginning of a relative decline of Dutch investment in English stocks. But at its height, in the 1750s, the flow of funds from a wealthy and discriminating Dutch bourgeoisie was a striking testimony to the security as well as the profitability of English funds, and a significant tribute to the English achievement.

Conclusion

In 1666, when he was laying foundations for the financial revolution, Sir George Downing had written to Pepys and promised, 'You shal see this business go on to that height that Holland shall not outgoe us in point of Credite. This is a great vow but by God's assistance you shal see it.' Downing, who died in 1684, did not live to see anything of the kind, but Pepys (1633–1708) was to survive the heroic years of that revolution and witness some of the remarkable achievements of the 1690s. Later, in the course of the eighteenth century, Downing's highest hopes were to be exceeded. Aggressive patriot that he was, with ambitions for England's aggrandisement in almost every corner of the globe, even he could not have imagined the plenitude of commercial and military power to which Great Britain had attained by the 1760s. Standing at the zenith of its first Empire it seemed to have vindicated the most febrile hopes of an earlier generation which, mired in its French and Dutch wars, had dreamed of financial salvation.

Was it then, 'a revolution'? Protracted, hesitant, marred by crisis though it was, the development of banking, borrowing, credit and investment in these 100 years has every entitlement to be matched in importance with the Industrial Revolution yet to come. For its significance was profound and is to be measured not merely by a buoyant National Debt, or a declining rate of interest, let alone in terms of battles won and empires gained. It is to be found in more subtle but pervasive achievements – in the peaceful interchange of a commercial community, the secure prosperity of a middling class and, perhaps most importantly, in the political stability of a nation acquiescent in its fiscal system and trustful of its public credit [**doc. 20**]. Revolutionary or not, the most important thing about the achievement is that it was always more than merely 'financial'.

Part Four: Documents

document 1
Shakespeare's England is introduced to the concept of 'a Bank'

Writing in the reign of James I, Gerard de Malynes set out to describe current European mercantile institutions and practices, including public (as distinct from private) banking.

Of Bankes and Bankers.
A Banke is properly a collection of all the readie money of some Kingdome, Common-Wealth, or Province, as also of a particular Citie or Towne, into the hands of some persons licensed and established thereunto by publicke authoritie of some King, Prince or Commonwealth, erected with great solemnitie in the view of all the people and inhabitants ... to persuade and allure the common people to bring their money into these Bankers hands, where at all times they may command it, and have it againe at their owne pleasure, with allowing them onely a small matter of five upon everie thousand ducats or crownes ...

Gerard de Malynes, *Consuetudo vel Lex Mercatoria*, 1622.

document 2
Charles II and his bankers

*In his autobiographical account of the years 1660–67, the Earl of Clarendon described approvingly the manner in which the King and his bankers reached agreement on loans, secured upon his revenues, at a generous rate of interest. His purpose was to stress the moral and constitutional value of the King's personal credit, in contrast to the later system of borrowing, guaranteed by parliamentary credit, and introduced by Sir George Downing in 1665 [**doc. 3**].*

The bankers did not consist of above the number of five or six men, some whereof were aldermen, and had been lord mayors of London, and all the rest were aldermen, or had fined for aldermen.[1] They were a tribe that had risen and grown up in Cromwell's time, and never heard of before the late troubles, till when the whole trade of money had passed through the hands of the scriveners: they were for the most part goldsmiths, men known to be so rich, and of so good reputation, that all the money of the kingdom would be trusted or deposited in their hands . . .

The method of proceeding with them was thus. As soon as an act of parliament was passed, the king sent for those bankers, (for there was never any contract made with them but in his majesty's presence:) and being attended by the ministers of the revenue, and commonly the chancellor [*i.e. Clarendon*] and others of the council, the lord treasurer presented a particular information to the king of the most urgent occasions for present money, either for disbanding troops, or discharging ships, or setting out fleets, (all of which are to be done together, and not by parcels;) so that it was easily foreseen what ready money must be provided. And this account being made, the bankers were called in, and told, 'that the king had occasion to use such a sum of ready money within such a day; they understood the act of parliament, and so might determine what money they could lend the king, and what manner of security would best satisfy them.' Whereupon one said, 'he would within such a time pay one hundred thousand pounds,' another more, and another less, as they found themselves provided; for there was no joint stock amongst them, but every one supplied according to his ability. They were desirous to have eight [*per cent interest*] in the hundred, which was not unreasonable to ask, and the king was 'willing to give:' but upon better consideration amongst themselves, they thought fit to decline that demand, as being capable of turning to their disadvantage, and would leave the interest to the king's own bounty, declaring 'that themselves paid six in the hundred for all the money with which they were intrusted,' which was known to be true.

Then they demanded such a receipt and assignment to be made to them by the lord treasurer, for the payment of the first money that should be payable upon that act of parliament, or a branch of that act, or tallies upon the farmers of the customs or excise, or such other branches of the revenue as were least charged; having the

---

[1] I.e., they had been elected as Aldermen but had resigned on payment of a fine. Thus, John Colville, one of Charles II's principal bankers, paid £720 to be discharged from his election in 1669.

king's own word and the faith of the treasurer, that they should be exactly complied with; for, let the security be what they could desire, it would still be in the power of the king or of the lord treasurer to divert what was assigned to them to other purposes. Therefore there is nothing surer, than that the confidence in the king's justice, and the unquestionable reputation of the lord treasurer's honour and integrity, was the true foundation of that credit which supplied all his majesty's necessities and occasions; and his majesty always treated those men very graciously, as his very good servants, and all his ministers looked upon them as very honest and valuable men. And in this manner, for many years after his majesty's return, even to the unhappy beginning of the Dutch war [*in 1665*], the public expenses were carried on ... and nobody opened his mouth against the bankers, who every day increased in credit and reputation, and had the money of all men at their disposal.

(**4**), vol. II, pp. 192–3. My interpolations are italicised.

document 3
Sir George Downing introduces his scheme, 1665

Writing in exile, the Earl of Clarendon gives a valuable but deeply hostile account of Downing (1623–84) and the historic introduction of his visionary scheme to attract loans to the Exchequer from the general public with parliamentary guarantees of prompt repayment, with interest, in a strict chronological sequence which neither the King nor his ministers could interfere with.

There was a man who hath been often named, sir George Downing, who by having been some years in the office of one of the tellers of the exchequer,[1] and being of a restless brain, did understand enough of the the nature of the revenue and of the course of the receipt, to make others who understood less of it to think that he knew the bottom of it, and that the expedients, which should be proposed by him towards a reformation, could not but be very pertinent and practicable. ... He was a member of parliament, and a very voluminous speaker, who would be thought wiser in trade than any of the merchants, and to understand the mystery of all professions much better than the professors of them.

---

[1] One of the four senior Exchequer officials in charge of the receipt and issue of money.

[*Downing*] enlarged more in discourse, and told [*the King and his Council*]

'that this [*would be an*] encouragement to lend money, by making the payment with interest so certain and fixed, that there could be [*no*] security in the kingdom like it, when it should be out of any man's power to cause any money that should be lent to-morrow to be paid before that which was lent yesterday, but that should be infallibly paid in order; by which the exchequer (which was now bankrupt and without any credit) would be quickly in that reputation, that all men would deposit their money there: and that he hoped in few years, by observing the method he now proposed, he would make his exchequer the best and the greatest bank in Europe, and where all Europe would, when it was once understood, pay in their money for the certain profit it would yield, and the indubitable certainty that they should receive their money.'

And with this discourse the vain man, who had lived many years in Holland, and would be thought to have made himself master of all their policy, had amused the king ..., undertaking to erect the king's exchequer into the same degree of credit that the bank of Amsterdam [*stood upon*], the institution whereof he undertook to know, and from thence to make it evident, 'that all that should be transplanted into England, and all nations would sooner send their money into the exchequer, than into Amsterdam or Genoa or Venice.' And it cannot be enough wondered at, that this intoxication prevailed so far, that no argument would be heard against it ...

And though it was made [*to*] appear, by very solid arguments, that the imagination of a bank was a mere chimera in itself, and the erecting it in the exchequer must suppose that the crown must be always liable to a vast debt upon interest, which would be very ill husbandry ... yet all discourse against a bank was thought to proceed from pure ignorance. And sir George [*Downing*] was let loose to instruct them how easy it was to be established, who talked imperiously 'of the method by which it came to be settled [*in Holland*] by the industry of very few persons, when the greatest men despaired of it as impracticable; yet the obstinacy of the other prevailed, and it was now become the strength, wealth, and security of the state: that the same would be brought to pass much more easily here, and would be no sooner done, than England would be the seat of all the trade of Christendom.' And then assuming all he said to be demonstration, he wrapped himself up, according to his custom, in a mist of words that nobody could see light in, but they who by often hearing the same chat thought they understood it.

(**4**), vol. II, pp. 190–1. My interpolations are italicised.

document 4
Samuel Pepys borrows £1,000 on a Treasury Order

A rare surviving example of an early Treasury Order was issued to Pepys as treasurer for the Tangiers garrison. It was an 'imprest' – Exchequer jargon for an allocation – of £1,000, due to be paid eventually from a current tax. Signed by the Chancellor of the Exchequer, Lord Ashley, and another Treasury Lord, and counter-signed by a senior Exchequer official, Sir Robert Howard, it typifies the kind of securities issued by the government to its departments in lieu of cash, obliging them to borrow money on them as best they could. In this instance Pepys was lucky enough to get Edward Backwell, a leading banker, to cash Order No. 88, shortly before the 'Stop of the Exchequer' and on the back is his signed endorsement, assigning it to Backwell who in turn assigned it to others. (The original document is approximately 34 cm. × 24 cm.; handwritten insertions in the printed text are here italicised.)

88

Order is taken this ***xxx**^th **day of June 1671*** By vertue of His Majesties Letters of Privy Seal, dated this xith day of April, 1665, That you deliver and pay of such His Majesties Treasure as is or shall be remaining in your charge, unto Samuel Pepys Esquire, Receiver of the Moneys for the use of His Majesties City, Port and Garrison of Tangier, or to his Assigns, the sum of **One Thousand Pounds** by way of Imprest, and upon Accompt for his Majesties Garrison of the said City of Tangier, and for raising a Mole or Harbor there; and other Services in the said Privy Seal expressed. And these, together with his, or his Assignes, Acquittance, shall be your discharge herein.

Ashley
Duncombe

To be registered and paid out of the fourth q[ua]rt[er]ly payment of the late Subsidie granted to his Matie.

Ro. Howard
July 29.

Public Record Office, London: Exchequer records E.407/120.

document 5
The origins of deposit banking: (a) the public sector

These extracts are taken from an anonymous attack on the goldsmith-bankers, which typifies widespread hostility to their emergence. Published in 1676, it was probably government-inspired to excuse Charles II's 'Stop of the Exchequer' of 1672, which temporarily ruined the bankers' business, and as an account of the origins of English deposit-banking during the Civil War it should not be taken too literally.

But about Thirty years since, the Civil Wars giving opportunity to Apprentices to leave their Masters at will, and the old way having been for Merchants to trust their Cash in one of their Servants custody, many such Cashiers left their Masters in the lurch and went to the Army, and Merchants knew not how to confide in their Apprentices; then did some Merchants begin to put their Cash into Goldsmiths hands to receive and pay for them, (thinking it more secure) and the trade of Plate being then but little worth, most of the Nobility and Gentry, and others melting down their old Plate rather then buying new, and few daring to use or own Plate, the Goldsmiths sought to be the Merchants Cash-keepers to receive and pay for nothing, few observing or conjecturing their profit they had for their pains.

The Goldsmiths found a new Mischeivous trade to send all the money trusted in their hands into their Cocklofts, where they had Scales and various Weights adapted for their pourpose, and servants constantly weighed every half-crown (at least) and sorted them to melt for Two pence or three pence, or sometimes less gain by the ounce, and sometimes their advantage being greater by the accidents of the rise or fall of the exchange, those heaviest Coins were sent away in specie, several French men and other Merchants making it their whole and only business weekly to transport the gold and silver so culled, either melted down or in specie; and from hence the Goldsmiths set up another new Trade of buying the old English gold coin at a rate much above its Lawful coyned value, buying and selling it at five, seven, eight and ten pounds in the hundred more than it was coyned for . . .

These unlawful practices and profits of the Goldsmiths, made them greedy to ingross all the Cash they could, and to combine with all mens servants who continued to keep any Cash, to bring their moneys to them to be culled, and to remain with them at four pence the day interest per centum without the Masters privity: And having thus got Money into their hands, they presumed upon some to come as fast as others was paid away; and upon that confidence of a running Cash (as they call it) they begun to accommodate men with moneys for Weeks and Moneths upon extraordinary gratuities, and supply all necessitous Merchants that over traded their Stock, with present Money for their Bills of Exchange, discounting sometimes double, perhaps treble interest for the time as they found the Merchant more or less pinched.

Profit arising by this Trade, some of them who had the highest Credit, undertook to receive Gentlemens Rents as they were returned to Town, and indeed any Man's money, and to allow them some intrest for it though it lay for a month only, or less, the Owners calling for it by a hundred or fifty pounds at a time as their occasions and expences wanted it; this new practice giving hopes to every body to make Profit of their money until the hour they spent it, and the conveniency as they thought, to command their money when they pleased, which they could not do when lent at intrest upon personall or reall Security; These hopes I say, drew a great Cash into these new Goldsmiths hands, and some of them stuck to their old Trade, but every of them that had friends and credit, aspired to this new Mystery to become Bankers or Casheers, and when Cromwell usurped the Government, the greatest of them began to deal with him to supply his wants of Money upon great Advantages . . .

After the King's return he wanting money, some of these Bankers undertook to lend him not their own but other mens money, taking barefaced of Him ten pounds for the hundred, and by private contracts many Bills, Orders, Tallies and Debts of the King's, above twenty, and sometimes thirty in the hundred, to the great dishonour of the Government.

This Prodigious unlawful Gain induced all of them that could be credited with moneys at intrest to become lenders to the King to anticipate all the Revenue, to take every Grant of the Parliament into pawn as soon as it was given . . . and to outvie each other in buying and taking to pawn, Bills, Orders, and Tallies, in effect all the King's revenue passed into their hands, and if Solomon be in the right, that the Borrower is a Slave to the Lender, the King and Kingdom became Slaves to these Bankers, and the Kingdom gave no small share of their Taxes to them, paying double and treble Intrest, as if they had not been able to raise Money for the publick Service at the times it was requisite.

The Mystery of the New Fashioned Goldsmiths or Bankers, 1676, reprinted in (**24**), pp. 684–7.

document 6
The origins of deposit banking: (b) the private sector

After nearly twenty years abroad, making his fortune in the Levant, Sir Dudley North (1641–91) returned to England in 1680 to discover the disagreeable novelty of goldsmith-bankers, touting for the privilege of holding his current account, or 'running cash'. Unwisely, he initially chose to entrust money to Hinton, who went bankrupt in 1684, but he was shrewder in his later choice of Child's bank, which still conducts business at No. 1 Fleet Street today.

He found divers usages in London very different from what had been practised, in his time, there, or in any other place where he had lived: as, first, touching their running cash, which, by almost all sorts of merchants, was slid into goldsmiths' hands; and they themselves paid and received only by bills; as if all their dealings were *in banco*. He counted this a foolish, lazy method, and obnoxious to great accidents; and he never could bring himself wholly to comply with it. For, having taken an apprentice . . . he paid and received all by his cash-keeper, in his own counting-house, as merchants used to do. But, at length, he was prevailed on to use Benjamin Hinton, a Lombard-street man; and, for acting therein against his conscience, was punished with the loss of about fifty pounds. But others lost great sums by this man; and his breaking made a great shake upon the Exchange. I remember, he hath come home . . . in great amazement at his own greatness; for the banking goldsmiths came to him upon the Exchange, with low obeisances, 'hoping for the honour' – 'should be proud to serve him,' and the like; and all for nothing but to have the keeping of his cash. This pressing made him the more averse to that practice; and, when his acquaintance asked him where he kept his cash, he said, 'at home; where should he keep it?' They wondered at him, as one that did not know his own interest. But, in the latter end of his time, when he had left the city, and dealt more in trusts and mortgages, than in merchandize, he saw a better bottom, and used the shop of Sir Francis Child, at Temple-bar, for the paying and receiving all his great sums.

The Lives of the Norths by Roger North, London, 1826, vol. III, pp. 102–3.

English v. Dutch finance, 1678–80 document 7

In this series of letters, Sidney Godolphin advises William of Orange how best to invest in English securities. Godolphin, who was to serve both William III and Queen Anne at the head of the Treasury and was now a Junior Lord, naturally draws attention to the merits of Treasury securities but also names the two most powerful private financiers in England, the goldsmith-banker Charles Duncombe and the courtier Sir Stephen Fox. William, familiar with lower interest returns but better security in the Netherlands, was evidently not impressed.

(a)   I doe not find it practicable to gett your H[ighnes]s money secured, either by merchants in Holland or by merchants in London, but there is a goldsmith in London, one Mr Duncomb, who is a man in great creditt, that will take this sum of money at 6 pr cent, and give your Highnesse his bond, to pay it at any time upon three months warning. This is the best private security that can bee gotten; if your Highnesse likes better to accept of security upon the Kings revenue, you may have 8 per cent; but you cannot bee at liberty to have your money at soe short warning . . .

(b)   By the last I had the honour to receive from your Highness, I find you still persist to have merchants security for your mony, and are unwilling to accept of Mr Duncombe, who, I confesse, is noe merchant, but is a banquier of the best creditt that ever has been in England, and is able to answer for as much money, or more, than any three merchants upon the Exchange of London; his bonds your Highnesse may have, with liberty to withdraw your whole summ, or any part of it, at 3 months warning and interest at 6 per cent, for as long as you shall think fitt to leave it in his hands. This is as good private security as is to bee had in England, and . . . as long as the treasury continus under the management of those who have now the honour to bee employ'd in it, your money would bee as well secur'd to you upon the Kings revenue as upon any private security whatsoever, and that way you might have 8 per cent for itt; from Mr Duncomb you can have but six.

(c)   I did not think to have troubled your Highnesse any more concerning your money, since you seemed to resolve not to leave your money in any banquiers hands here, without caution given you at the same time from merchants in Holland, for the payment of itt in

3 months time, but, it being very unusuall' for merchants to enter into any engagements of that nature, it was not practicable to obtayn that security which your Highnesse seem'd most to desire, and therefore I had left off the thoughts of making any more propositions to you, till within these 2 days I have been offer'd a security which I think extreamly good ... It is this; Sir Steven Fox, who besides his employements has an estate in land of at least 4000£, a yeare, does offer mee to receive your Highnesses money here, as it comes into the Exchecquer, and to give his owne bond for the repayment of it that day' twelvemonth with interest at 6 per cent.

(d)   Since my last, wherein I proposed to your Highnesse Sir Ste. Fox's security for your money (in case you would leave it in Engeland), I have not had the honour of any letter from you, but expect every day to heare from your Highnesse upon it ... I have been inform'd (how truly I know not) that at this time no body gives more than 4 per cent for money in Holland; if it bee soe, your Highnesse may certainly dispose of it here to much more advantage; for you may have 6 per cent with as good personall security as any is in England; you may have 8 per cent and bee secured upon the Kings *hereditary* revenue, which gives you as good a title in law as any man can have in England, though you had no trust at all in the Com[issioners] of the Treasury; but as long as wee continue who have the honour to bee employd there now, I dare confidently say you run no kind of hazard neither one way, nor tother, but indeed, if it were my own case, I should take 8 per cent and think myselfe very secure upon the Kings revenue.

(a) March 1678 (b) 4 May 1680 (c) 1 June 1680 (d) 15 June 1680

Archives ou correspondance inédite de la maison d'Orange-Nassau, ed. Groen van Prinsterer, Leyden & Utrecht, 1861, 2nd series, vol. 5, pp. 365, 397–8, 402, 405–6.

document 8
The debate on the king's revenue, 1690

In this debate in the House of Commons, on 27 March 1690, the fundamental dilemma was faced, whether to grant a revenue adequate for William III to fight the war or one insufficient to give the crown a dangerous independence. Among those contributing were Members (such as Foley and Williamson) who had served in Parliament since the 1660s and were reluctant to repeat the mistakes made at the Restoration of Charles II and the accession of James II.

Mr Paul Foley.] What you are now debating is of vast consequence to us, and England, for ever. I would know what the Revenue is, and what it is likely to prove, and not to settle a Revenue for Life, as is necessary in War, but in time of Peace. When Charles II returned, it was generally agreed, that 1,200,000£ *per annum*, was a sufficient Revenue to support the Government ... I know not what the Revenue is now; but I have heard, that in Charles II's time, it was two Millions, and more in King James's time; therefore, I would have you consider, and it is worth your while to consider: If you settle such a Revenue, as that the King should have no need of a Parliament, I think we do not our duty to them that sent us hither. Therefore I would know what the Revenue is.

Sir Edmund Jennings.] I remember the method in King James's Parliament, and why now we should take other Precedents, I know not. If you desire to preserve the Church and State, will you not settle such a Revenue as will do it, and why is not this King to be trusted as well as King James? Either we shall run back to Popery and Slavery on the one hand, or Anarchy on the other. What will neighbouring Princes say, if we do not by this Prince, as we have done by the former? ...

Mr Hutchinson.] You have been moved 'to settle a Revenue upon this King, as upon King James.' I would know whether that had so good effect, as to settle it so now, and whether so extravagant a Grant can be good either for a good or a bad Prince? If you gave this Revenue to a bad Prince, you cannot now decently take it away; if you give it to a good Prince, he may be thrifty, and may have a Bank, and may presume upon it to destroy our Liberties ...

Mr Pelham.] You are told 'that the Revenue came to two Millions in King Charles's and King James's time;' but, as to what is said of the ill effects of it in King James's time, none of that mischief came by that Revenue, but upon what was given him afterwards, which enabled him to raise his Army, and bring in Popery.

Sir Joseph Williamson.] ... A Supply is necessary; we cannot sit here else. A Revenue for the King to live with honour and comfort upon, every body is for, so as to provide for the Monarchy, in whose hands soever it is, that Parliaments may be frequent. There are some alive, that know all, and have felt, that, when Princes have not needed Money, they have not needed us.

(**12**), vol. 10, pp. 10–11.

document 9
The idea of long-term borrowing is introduced, 1692

In these debates in the House of Commons, (a) on 9 January, and (b) on 15 December 1692, Members of Parliament begin to contemplate the idea of long-term borrowing as a less painful alternative to a poll-tax. In (a), as a senior Lord of the Treasury Sir John Lowther is proposing that, in return for a large loan from the public, the government should set up a board of trustees which would issue interest-bearing notes as legal tender, an idea in which one can discern the seeds of the Bank of England. In (b), the indefatigable 'projector', Thomas Neale, introduces an alternative scheme which is brushed aside in favour of a 'tontine' – a gamble on life-expectation.

(a)   *Sir John Lowther*: If the House be at leisure to hear a proposal, I think there is that which may be better than this of a poll bill and that is raising a fund for perpetual interest. I have heard the reasons for the same and it has convinced me. It is this: that there should be a fund for perpetual interest at five per cent and this settled on trustees; that their bills of credit or paper be current and all obliged to take them; and that from the very time such bills are given he shall have interest at five per cent without paying any taxes and without any further charge. I believe this will be for the advantage of the public, and is not like brass or leather money but like to a mortgage and as good – which may be assigned over. A man may part with it easier than the land, both for the revenue it brings in and for the advantage in parting with it. It is more beneficial to the merchant, trader, grazier, etc. I would also have the Crown obliged to take it in taxes or other payments, and it will be no prejudice to any for I may transfer it over. It is objected by some that this will not pay daughters' portions or debts. Why not, if it be transferable and gain credit? It is that which will establish it, like goldsmiths' notes which are as good as so much ready money. This proposal has also this advantage; while ready money lies dead by a man and yields nothing, these bills will yield five per cent and avoid paying great interest to the bankers. Thus the whole tax is raised at once, paying about £60,000 per annum for interest and that one of the ninepences on the excise will do.

Mr Neale: I think this a very good project and the more it is considered I believe the better it will be liked.

Mr Hampden: I think this proposal a very dishonourable reflection on the English nation that can be and very impracticable. It will be prejudicial to trade in putting a stop to the same and will have such mischiefs attending it as can't be imagined.

Sir Ralph Carr: I am for this proposal, and take it in a little time after its erection when it hath gained credit and it will be as good as the bank in Holland.

Sir John Knight: This is not the least like that of Holland. There if you do not like your note, you may have it in ready money what you have occasion for, but in this there is no ready money.

(b) *Mr Neale*: There is a way to raise money without paying so much interest as you do on all your taxes – by settling a perpetual fund of £120,000 to pay the interest of £2,000,000. This will tend to strengthen your government by interesting so many persons to wish well to it and to endeavour to preserve it. I shall propose the fund to be on the hereditary excise and to lay 1*s* a bushel on all salt made at the pan and 2*s* a bushel on all foreign salt, and you may for further security give a clause of credit as you did on the poll act.

Mr Paul Foley: I cannot agree to anything of a perpetual fund, for you can have no fruit of that unless you will force tallies or paper to go for ready money. But I will propose you a thing for a certain fund of £70,000 per annum. You shall have persons raise you a million of money, they to have £6 per annum for every £100, and if anyone die his share to be divided amongst the survivors. This fund to be upon the hereditary excise. He that lives longest will have a mighty return for his money. It is a good provision for children and no burden on your land. Herein also I would give a clause of credit.

Mr Harley: I approve of this very well, and though some may say it will not come to that sum, yet you will reap this advantage by it that you will have one year more to consider how to raise the sum.

Sir Thomas Clarges: Of all the new ways to raise money I think this the best, and therefore I am for it. But there must be great care taken in the penning of the act.

Sir Christopher Musgrave: I think this a very good thing and a careful provision for children, and therefore I am for it.

Sir Edward Seymour for the same, it being but trying an experiment which hath the appearance of reason. And though it has not been tried in this nation, yet it has elsewhere and taken very well . . .

So the question was stated by the Chair, put and resolved: That

towards the supply to be granted to Their Majesties there be a fund
of £70,000 per annum set apart for the payment of the interest of a
million of money to be raised by persons voluntarily paying in that
sum; the principal paid in to be sunk and the persons paying in the
same to receive during their lives their respective proportions of the
said £70,000 according to the sums paid in by them, with the advantage of survivorship till all the lives be determined.

(**13**), pp. 140, 321–3.

document 10
A beginner's guide to dealing in stocks and shares, 1694

In June 1694, John Houghton began to describe to the readers of his Collection
for Improvement of Husbandry and Trade *how to speculate in stocks
and shares. Surprisingly, he starts by describing the risky process of betting
for, or against, the rise or fall of the market, by purchasing an 'option' to buy
at a specified price. For an explanation of these technicalities see pp. 66–7
above.*

(a)   The manner of managing the Trade is this; The Monied Man
goes among the Brokers (which are chiefly upon the Exchange, and
at Jonathan's Coffee House, sometimes at Garaway's, and at some
other Coffee Houses) and asks how Stocks go? and upon Information, bids the broker buy or sell so many Shares of such and such
Stocks if he can, at such and such Prizes;[1] Then he tries what he
can do among those that have stock, or power to sell them; and if
he can, makes a Bargain.

Another time he asks what they will have for Refuse of so many
Shares: That is, how many Guinea's[2] a Share he shall give for liberty to Accept or Refuse such Shares, at such a price, at any time
within Six Months, or other time they shall agree for.

For instance; when [East] India [Company] Shares are at Seventy
Five, some will give Three Guinea's a Share, Action,[3] or Hundred
Pound, down for Refuse at Seventy Five, any time within Three

---

[1] Prices.
[2] The gold 'Guinea' – so called because it was first minted in 1663 with
gold from Guinea in W. Africa – could vary in value, but was originally
worth 21*s* in silver.
[3] Like many other terms used on the early stock-market, 'action' was borrowed from Dutch – in this case, '*actie*', meaning a bond or share.

Months, by which means the Accepter of the Guinea's, if they be not called for in that time, has his Share in his own Hand for his Security; and the Three Guinea's, which is after the rate of Twelve Guinea's profit in a Year for Seventy Five Pound, which he could have sold for at the Bargain making if he had pleased; and in time, tho' they should fall still lower, unless he will run the hazard of buying again at any rate if they should be demanded; by which many have been caught and paid dear for, as you shall see afterwards: So that if Three Months they stand at a stay, he gets the Three Guinea's, if they fall so much, he is as he was, losing his Interest, and whatever they fall lower is loss to him.

But if they happen to rise in that time Three Guinea's, and the charge of Brokerage, Contract and Expence, then he that paid the Three Guinea's demands the Share, pays the Seventy Five Pounds, and saves himself. If it rises but one or two Guinea's, he secures so much, but whatever it rises to beyond what it cost him, is Gain.

(b)   Another part relating to Stock is PUTTING; that is, when they give so many Guinea's to some to have Liberty to PUT upon them, that is, to make them take and pay the Money agreed for so many Shares, at such a Price in such or such a Time. For instance, When the East-India Shares, Actions, or Hundred Pounds are worth each Seventy Five Pounds, some who have occasion for Money will sell to another, who for hopes of Gain will buy, if he can be assured he shall have no great loss; therefore the Seller, to incourage his Customer, will, for a Guinea and a half (more or less as they agree) oblige himself to take the Action again at the same Price he sold it for, at any time within Three Months, if he that bought will Put it upon him, that is, will demand of him so to do; by which means he is sure (having a good Man to deal with) he can lose but his Guinea and a half (or Summ agreed for) and the Interest of his Money, besides Brokage, and petty Charges: Upon this Score both Parties are pleased, the one ventures his Guinea and a half, and Interest for the hopes of a great Gain, and the other for the Guinea and a half, and Interest, runs all the hazard of all the loss shall happen in the time, and has the others Money to make use of to any other purpose he shall think will be advantageous to him.

By this means many are incouraged to come into new Stocks, the success whereof is very uncertain; and it is also possible that when the Seller himself is diffident of its holding up, he will do this in a few Shares, because it will make the Market price at such a rate, at which many others will buy, running the hazard without ensuring themselves, as aforesaid, which if many do, the Seller puts off his Shares at a good Price, and does not then care how much it falls, that at a low rate he may again buy, and take his fortune for raising it again. And thus in small Stocks 'tis possible to have Shares rise or fall by the Contrivances of a few Men in Confederacy; but in great Stocks 'tis with more difficulty.

(**14**), (a) 22 June 1694; (b) 6 July 1694.

document 11

The Bank of England defended, 1695

Shortly before he was killed at the siege of Namur, Michael Godfrey — a director of the Bank of England — explained how the new institution was helping to bring down the cost of official borrowing by reducing the rate of interest and removing the discount or 'premio' which had meant that government IOUs ('Tallies') used to be worth 15 to 30 per cent less than their face value. He also alludes to the social and political benefits brought by the Bank.

The Bank, besides the raising £1,200,000 towards the Charge of the War, cheaper than it could otherwise have been done, (and like the other Publick Funds, tying the People faster to the Government) will infallibly lower the Interest of Money; as well on Publick as Private Securities, which all other Funds have advanced, and which hath been raised to an Exorbitant Rate, as to the Publick, by those who have made use of its Necessities, and are now angry at the Bank, because that will reduce it. And the lowering of Interest, besides the Encouragement it will be to Industry and Improvements, will by a natural consequence raise the Value of Land, and encrease Trade, both which depend upon it; but it cannot be expected that Land should rise much whilst such high Taxes continue upon it, and whilst there are so great advantages to be made by lending Money to the Publick.

The Bank gives Money for Tallies on Funds, having a Credit of Loan by Act of Parliament, and which are payable in 2 years time, for the growing Interest only, without any other Allowance, on which there was used to be paid for the Change, as much or more than the Publick Interest: For even on the Land Tax, which is counted the best of all the Funds, there has been frequently given on Tallies payable in 3 or 4 Months time, 1, $1\frac{1}{2}$, $1\frac{3}{4}$ and 2 per cent. premio, over and above the Publick Interest; and Tallys on some Funds, on which but 12 or 18 Months past there was £25 and £30 per cent. given over and above the Publick Interest, are now taken by the Bank for nothing . . .

Thus by a regular course, and without any violence, the Bank has made Tallys currant in Payment, which is what has been so long wisht for, but could not have been effected without the Bank, (although there had been a Law to compel it), and this has given such a Reputation to all Tallys, even those which are the most remote, that they are now currantly taken by private persons at 6, 8, 10, 15, and 20 per cent less allowance than what was given but some few Months before the Bank was Establisht . . .

The more Credit the Bank has, and the more Money is lodged in it, the more it will lessen Interest, for want of Occasions to improve it; and those who lodge their Money in the Bank have it as much at their disposal as if it were in the hands of the Goldsmiths, or in their own Cash-Chest, and there is a greater Value than the Money which is deposited in the Bank that circulates by their Credit as much as if it were stirring in Specie: And the Bank-Bills serve already for Returns and Exchange to and from the Remotest parts of the Kingdom, and will in a little time do the like in Foreign Parts, which will lessen the exporting Bullion for the paying and maintaining our Armies abroad during this War; and if the Bulk of the Money of the Nation which has been Lodged with the Goldsmiths, had been deposited in the Bank 4 or 5 years past, it had prevented its being so Scandalously Clipt, which one day or other must cost the Nation a Million and half, or Two Millions to Repair.

The Bank will reduce the Interest of Mony in England to 3 per cent. per an. in a few years, without any Law to enforce it, in like manner as it is in all other Countreys where Banks are Establisht, whereby the Trade of the Nation may be driven upon more equal Terms with the rest of our Neighbours, where Mony is to be had at so much lower Rates than what we in England have hitherto paid: And as the lessening the Interest of Mony will Infallibly raise the Value of Land, it had been worth while for the Nobility and Gentry who are the Proprietors of the Real Estates in England, to have given a Land Tax for the Bank, of double the Sum which was raised by it, if they could not otherwise have obtained it; for the falling the Interest of Mony to 3 per cent. per annum, to which Rates the Bank will reduce it, will unavoidably advance the Price of Land to above 30 years Purchase,[1] which will raise the Value of Lands in England

---

[1] I.e., raise the market price of land to 30 times its annual rental value. In the 1690s freehold land was selling for about 20–21 'years purchase'.

at least 100 Millions, and thereby abundantly reimburse the Nation all the Charges of the War, and will not only enable the Gentry to make better Provision for their Younger Children, but those who now owe Money on their Lands, to pay off their Debts, by the Increase of the Value of their Estates.

The Ease and Security of the great Receipts and Payments of Mony which are made by the Bank, (where Peoples Cash is kept as it is at the Goldsmiths) together with the safe depositing of it, are such advantages to recommend it, that they ought not to be past over without some Observation; especially considering how much Mony has been lost in England by the Goldsmiths and Scriveners Breaking,[2] which in about 30 Years past, cannot amount to so little as betwixt Two and Three Millions, all which might have been prevented, had a Bank been sooner Establisht . . .

Michael Godfrey, *A Short Account of the Bank of England*, 1695.

[2] 'Breaking' meant being declared bankrupt.

document 12
The virtues of a 'Land-Bank' extolled, 1695

Dr Hugh Chamberlen, formerly physician to Charles II and member of a distinguished medical family who invented the midwifery forceps, was also a passionate advocate of a bank founded upon land-security. This extract comes from one of the many pamphlets he wrote on the subject, and in its concern for the landed gentry it conveys some of the contemporary Tory hostility to the recently founded Bank of England – 'the Royal Bank' – as well as the general antagonism between the interests of 'Land' and those of 'Money'.

Whereas at present, tho' the Landed-Man be never so willing to sell his Estate to pay his Debts, yet because he cannot get the Money, the Merciless Money'd Man takes the Advantage of him, seizeth his Estate, imprisoneth his Person, forecloseth the Equity of Redemption,[1] and leaves the miserable Landed-Man's Family to starve, and many Traders to suffer Loss, to whom he was indebted: And what, except killing the Man, can our Enemies the French do more? This proposal of Credit on Land, will heal the aforesaid Evils, and fully

[1] I.e., the creditor deprives the landowner-borrower of the equitable right of redeeming his debt and thus of his last chance of retaining occupation of the mortgaged property.

Answer all our present Necessities; there being now no other way
left that is possible to be found out. For the present Royal Bank
refuses to supply Mortgagers, tho' they offer'd it in their Advertise-
ments; and yet at the same time endeavour to engross all the Money
in the Nation to themselves; which makes the other Money'd Men
to put the more extravagant value on what they have; and this looks
as if they had all combined together to undermine the Landed-Men,
and seiz their Estates; and that this is carrying on, may be proved
by there being at this instant near Two hundred Bills for foreclosing
the Equity of Redemption. It is the Interest of Landed-Men therefore, and the only Remedy left, nay it is absolutely necessary for the
better support of their Families, and the preservation of the Value
of their Lands, to agree together with one Consent, and in their
Defence to run Counter to the Designs of all unfair Dealers in
Money, and to shake off their Slavery by engaging their Lands to
make good all Bills and Tickets of Credit that shall be given out
thereupon; and this will make Land perform the Use of Money, as
well as Gold and Silver when Coined. All Shopkeepers, and others
whatsoever, may more safely take them in payment, than the present
Royal Bank or Goldsmith's Notes; these having no other Fund to
make them good but their bare Reputation, which is nothing at all;
for if they Break, it is lost; if Dye, it is an hazard; but the Land is
the best and certainest Security the World can give: And by this
Means the Interest of Money will be lower'd, the Landed-Man
saved from Ruine, and Enabled to pay his Debts, and spend more
freely, to the great Encouragement of Trade: For as the Case now
stands, all our Land and Staple Commodities dance Attendance on
Money, made of a Foreign Commodity, and of which we can therefore have no certainty: for that the Industry, Cunning, or Caprice
of Foreign Princes and Merchants may not only debar its Entrance,
but draw away what we are already possess'd of . . . So that by
degrees the Landed-Men are eaten out of their Estates, for want of
having the Ballance kept even between Interest of Money, and Rents
of Land. But when once our Land shall be thus by Bills or Tickets
of Credit, turn'd into the Nature of Money, it may wait on Commodities, and serve all our Occasions full as well as Money.
Land-Banks have this Prerogative over all other Banks, viz. We are
sure none but English shall have the immediate benefit of them,
without any disobliging Exclusive Clauses. Whereas we can have no
Certainty that the Royal Bank of England doth not belong intirely
to Foreigners; 'tis sure a good part of it doth. Further, the Fund of
Land can never be imbezled, nor transported; but 'tis possible all

the Fund of Money'd Banks may be drawn out to Holland, France, or Constantinople, and nothing left to England . . .

A Proposal by Dr Hugh Chamberlen in Essex Street, for a Bank of Secure Current Credit To be Founded upon Land, 1695.

document 13
The new age of 'projecting' and financial speculation, 1695

*Alarmed that 'the poor English Nation runs a madding after new Inventions, Whims, and Projects', this anonymous writer denounced the contemporary mania for launching joint-stock ventures of questionable utility and doubtful integrity, among them the Bank of England, the Land Bank and the lotteries. For a more objective appraisal of this mania see Macleod (**131**) and Scott (**183**).*

A fair and clear Discovery of many crafty Cheats, and villainous Knaveries, will be of vast advantage to the Publick, in preserving each Individual from the Rock on which so many have split, and been undone. This Treatise will serve for a Buoy or Mark to the Nation, to beware how they are wheedled and drawn into these pernicious Projects following, viz. Banks – National, Land, Money, Paper or Notes, Orphans, &c, now on foot, and more preparing; Companies for Mines of Gold, Silver, Copper, Tin, Lead, Iron, Antimony, Lapis Caliminaris, &c. Coals, Salt-Rock, and other Engines innumerable; Diving of many sorts, to fish up Wreck, Guns, Tackle, Treasure, Merchandize, &c. Dipping, Japanning, Glass-Bottles, Venetian-Metal, Leather, Linen English, Scotch, New Jersey; Paper White, Blue, English, Irish; Japanned, Printed-Hangings, Pearl-fishing, Salt-Petre, Sword-Blades; Waters of the New River, Conduit, Thames, Hampstead, Shadwell, &c. Wrecks, South-Sea, Coasts of Spain, Portugal, France, England, Scotland, Ireland, and Holland; Lifting-Engines, Drawing-Engines, of several kinds, for Meares, Marshes, Inundations, Mines of all sorts, &c. Lutestring Company, Lotteries for Money or Merchandize; New Settlements in Carolina, Pensilvania, and Tobago, and other Parts; Convex-Lights, and others; Fisheries Royal and Private; Corporations or Companies of many kinds; Patents, Leases, Grants, &c. With some few more Projects now in Agitation.

Angliae Tutamen: or, The Safety of England. Being an Account of the Banks,

Lotteries, Mines, Diving, Draining, Lifting, and other Engines, and many pernicious Projects now on foot; tending to the Destruction of Trade and Commerce and the Impoverishing this Realm. By a Person of Honour, 1695.

document 14
Defoe describes the stock market, c. 1719

In this section from The Anatomy of Exchange Alley, *Defoe takes the reader for a short walk round the boundaries of the early stock market located in and near the two famous coffee-houses, Jonathan's and Garraway's.*

The Center of the Jobbing is in the Kingdom of Exchange-Alley, and its Adjacencies; the Limits are easily surrounded in about a Minute and a half (viz.) stepping out of Jonathan's into the Alley, you turn your Face full South, moving on a few Paces, and then turning Due East, you advance to Garraway's; from thence going out at the other Door, you go on still East into Birchin-Lane, and then halting a little at the Sword Blade Bank to do much mischief in fewest Words, you immediately face to the North, enter Cornhill, visit two or three petty provinces there in your way West: And thus having Box'd your Compass, and sail'd round the whole Stock-Jobbing Globe, you turn into Jonathan's again; and so, as most of the great Follies of Life oblige us to do, you end just where you began.

The Anatomy of Exchange-Alley: or, A System of Stock-Jobbing, Proving that Scandalous Trade, as it is now carry'd on, to be Knavish in its Private Practice, and Treason in its Publick . . . by A Jobber. [Daniel Defoe], London, 1719, p. 35.

document 15
The rise and fall of the South Sea 'Bubble', 1720

These extracts from the minutes of the South Sea Company's board of directors, ('the Court'), illustrate (1) the rapid rise, (2) the reckless climax, and (3) the ignominious collapse, of the Company's ambition to eclipse the Bank of England as a gigantic financial corporation.

1(a)   *Monday, 11th April 1720*
Resolved, Nem. Con. That a subscription be taken for sale of part

of the Capital Stock which this Company will be entitled to by virtue of the Act of Parliament.[1]

Resolved: That the said Subscription be opened at this House on Thursday next at 9 in the forenoon.

Resolved: That 1/5th part of the price for the Stock be paid to the Company's Cashier at the time of subscribing and the rest in 8 equal payments at 2 months distance from each other.

(b) *Wednesday, 13th April*

The Court taking into consideration what Price to sett on the Stock agreed by the Court the 11th instant to be sold tomorrow by Subscription, and also what quantity of Stock,

Resolved: That the Price for the Stock . . . be after the Rate of 300£ p. Cent.

Resolved: That the quantity of the Stock to be sold tomorrow by Subscription be Two Millions.

(c) *Thursday, 14th April*

Resolved, Nem. Con. That it is the opinion of this Court that the next Midsummer Dividend be made by 10 p. Cent on the Capital Stock of this Company, which the Company will be entitled to by virtue of the late Act of Parliament for increasing their Capital Stock.

(d) *Thursday, 21st April*

Resolved: That after reading the Minutes of the last General Court,[2] the Court be opened in the following manner, vizt. –

'Gentlemen. The Act being past for Enlarging the Capital Stock of this Company, your Court of Directors, in pursuance of the power you had lodged in them, thought it incumbent to begin the execution thereof by taking a subscription for sale of £2,250,000 Capital Stock at 300 p. Cent, of which 1/5th part is paid down, and the remaining four-fifths is to be paid in eight equal payments at two months distance from each other.

The money for this Subscription will, we believe, effectually enable the Company to go through with their undertaking, and if applied to pay off the Redeemables, the Company will be entitled thereby to an encreased Capital of £6,750,000 of which the present

---

[1] The Act of Parliament [6 Geo. I, c. 4] authorising the South Sea Company to seek the subscription of the National Debts into its capital, was given royal assent on 7 April.

[2] I.e., the shareholders' meeting.

purpose – To that degree of Lunacy are the People of this Age
arriv'd, that they'll be no where eased of the Burthen of their Cash,
but in Exchange-Alley; Twenty per Cent. is parted with for a bare
week's Loan of One Hundred Pounds, in Expectation of a Miser's
gain; (tho' the Consequence be farther loss;) and if Fame be not a
great Calumniator, some Persons of Distinction have generously
condescended to lay in Limbo their St[ar]s and G[arte]rs.[2]

When these extraordinary Events are consider'd, and Women of
the Town are become Dealers in the Stocks, Valets de Shambre,
Footmen and Porters (as well as Merchants, Tradesmen, and Pick-
pockets) walk on the Exchange, and ride in their Coaches, at the
same time some good natur'd Gentlemen have quitted them; Pro-
jectors successfully Bubble the Publick in all their Schemes; Sharpers
leave their Gaming-Tables in Covent-Garden, for more profitable
Business in Jonathan's Coffee-House; and even Poets commence
Stock-Jobbers, it is high time to pronounce Exchange-Alley truly a
FARCE.

From *Exchange-Alley: or the Stock-jobber turn'd Gentleman* (1720)

document 17
Stock-jobbing is attacked, and defended, 1733

In April 1733, lengthy speeches were made in the House of Commons for and
against a bill to outlaw 'the infamous practice of stockjobbing'. The bill was
wrecked by the House of Lords, but with support from Sir Robert Walpole
and Sir John Barnard it was passed in the following year.

(a)   *Mr Glanville*:] I am, Sir as great an enemy to stockjobbing as
any gentleman in this House, and for preventing that pernicious
practice I shall be glad to join in any measures, which are not destructive to public credit, and injurious to private persons, with
respect to the free use of their property: but, as I think the measures
proposed by this Bill will certainly be destructive of the one, and
injurious to the other, therefore I cannot let it pass, without taking
the liberty of offering my objections against it.

It is in all cases a great hardship put upon people, to subject them
to penalties, which may often by meer ignorance be incurred: but
in this case, the hardship is the greater, because there are many
proprietors of the public funds, particularly women, who cannot be

[2]That is, pawn their diamond-studded Order of the Garter.

presumed to be readers of acts of parliament: they put an entire confidence in their brokers, and, if the broker happens to neglect some of the forms prescribed, the most innocent persons may be brought under great penalties. Nay, I may say, that if this Bill passes into a law, it will always be in the power of any two or three brokers, to subject those that employ them to the severe penalties to be enacted by this Bill: for if two brokers should combine together, and enter in their books a bargain for time, as made between two of their correspondents, they might easily get a third person to combine with them, and to inform against the presumed buyer and seller . . .

(b)   *Sir John Barnard*:] The many bad consequences of stockjobbing are, I believe, well known; and that it is high time to put an end to that infamous practice, is, what I hope, most gentlemen in this House are convinced of. It is a lottery, or rather a gaming house, publicly set up in the middle of the city of London, by which the heads of our merchants and tradesmen are turned from getting a livelihood or an estate, by the honest means of industry and frugality; and are enticed to become gamesters by the hopes of getting an estate at once. It is, Sir, not only a lottery, but a lottery of the worst sort; because it is always in the power of the principal managers to bestow the benefit tickets as they have a mind. It is but lately since, by the arts and practices of stock jobbing, the East-India stock was run up to 200£ per cent. and in a little time after it tumbled down again below 150£.: several millions were lost and won by this single job,[1] and many poor men were undone; so bare-faced were some men at that time, in the infamous practice of stock jobbing, that, after that stock began to fall, they sold it cheaper for time than for ready money; which no man would have done, unless he had been made acquainted with the secret which came afterwards to be unfolded, but was then known to a very few . . .

This, Sir is a domestic evil; an evil which, though fatal in its consequences, yet does not perhaps immediately draw any money out of the nation; but there is a foreign evil attending the game of stock jobbing, by which the nation may be plundered of great sums of money at once. It is, by means of stock jobbing, always in the power

---

[1] East India Company stock was usually very stable in price, but between 1730 and 1733 it was shaken by doubts over the renewal of the Company's charter, the reduction of interest on its short-term bonds, and the restriction of its customary dividends by mismanagement in India. Some dealers may have taken advantage of this to buy cheaply.

Visiting the eighteenth-century Bank of England

By 1750 the Bank of England handled much of the day-to-day administration of the National Debt — recording stock-holdings, registering transfers and issuing dividends. For the novice investor this account gives a helpful guide to the Bank's many departments.

Directions to Strangers to find the several
Public Offices without Difficulty or Delay,

THE BANK

Entering at the front gateway in Threadneedle-street, facing Bank-buildings, Cornhill, you will see glass doors directly opposite, across a small court: They open into the GREAT HALL for transacting the common business of a banking-office, such as paying in money to be carried to account, and issued on demand; delivering notes for cash, or cash for notes; exchanging old for new notes; smaller for large, and the reverse; giving notices of notes lost or stolen; discounting of bills of exchange, &c.

If your business does not lie in that department, do not cross the court in a direct line, but look to the right angle, where you will see painted over a door, in large letters, the words

TRANSFER-OFFICES

This door leads to a passage, in which there is a small door on the right hand, inscribed *Office for unclaimed Dividends*. Proceeding along the passage, it opens into a rotunda, where the Brokers prepare their business previous to transacting it in the several offices.

On the right hand, over large glass doors, are painted the words

3 PER CENT. CONSOLIDATED ANNUITIES.

And in that office is a door, inscribed *Dividend Warrant Office*, leading to an interior apartment where the dividend warrants are delivered. On the left side is the office inscribed,

4 PER CENT. CONSOLIDATED, AND 5 PER CENT. NAVY.

Passing through the rotunda to an arch opposite to that by which you entered it, you may proceed to a passage which opens to Bartholomew-Lane. On the left in this passage is the office inscribed,

BANK-STOCK, LONG ANNUITIES, IMPERIAL ANNUITIES, IRISH ANNUITIES AND 5 PER CENT. 1797.

Returning back to the first court mentioned in these directions, and placing yourself in the same situation as at your first entry, you will observe in the centre of the left side of the court, a large portal, over which these words are conspicuous,

REDUCED ANNUITY OFFICE.

And on a side pillar,

3 PER CENT. 1726 AND SHORT ANNUITIES.

To these offices you pass along the side of a pretty garden; and on the left, before you enter them, there is a small door inscribed CHEQUER-OFFICE; but this does not concern the public; it is an office for checking the dividend warrants before and after they are paid.

(**20**) Appendix IV.

document 20
'Rule Britannia'. The National Debt = The National Credit

By the mid-eighteenth century, Englishmen had learned to take pride in the international reputation of their financial system. In these typical passages from a beginner's guide to the money markets, first issued in 1760 but in this edition dating from 1801, the author exults in the achievement.

(a)   The national credit of Great-Britain having long since arrived at the highest degree of reputation, and her securities for the loan of money being now esteemed the best in Europe, not only by her own subjects, but likewise by all unprejudiced foreigners; a full explanation of the nature of these securities deservedly merits the attention not only of the inhabitants of Great-Britain, but of all foreigners, on whom Providence has bestowed any portion of wealth, that is not employed in commerce, or laid out in landed estates; for where will they find so safe a repository for their money, and on such advantageous terms, as the Public Funds of England afford? Higher interest may indeed be obtained, but then the security is not so good.

Customs Government taxes, levied on imported and exported commodities at the ports, payable by merchants.

Discount (1) As a noun, a reduction of price (opposite of premium); (2) as a verb, to purchase at a lower price than the face value of a security.

Drafts Written demands for payment, in some forms the precursor of the cheque; thus the 'drawer' of a Bill of Exchange makes a draft on the 'payer'.

Endorsement A written amendment on a paper security, usually assigning its ownership to another named person.

Exchequer Bill Like a bank-note, a formal, printed 'promise-to-pay' first issued by the Exchequer in 1696 in convenient units and bearing interest. They were allowed to circulate, like currency, but only in payment of taxes and for only a limited period before being paid off and cancelled.

Excise Government taxation on commodities of domestic consumption – mainly liquor – and levied primarily on the producer or retailer.

'Floating debt' Government debts for repayment of which no specific parliamentary, or other, provision had been made. Periodically, large accumulations of such debt might be consolidated and provided with a source of repayment, or fund – and thus become 'funded debt'.

Flotation, floating The launching of a large-scale investment, such as a company or large loan, by a public appeal for subscriptions.

Funding The pledging or appropriation of revenue (funds) raised by parliamentary taxation to the payment of interest upon, and eventual repayment of, government debts.

Funds, The Loosely applied in the eighteenth and nineteenth centuries to the general array of government securities pledged to the payment of interest, and eventual principal.

'Gilt-edged' (slang). Used to describe an absolutely safe and reliable investment, usually in government stock.

Great Contract An unsuccessful scheme proposed by James I's ministers in 1610, by which it was hoped that his Parliament would grant the King a substantial increase in his permanent revenues in return for his surrender of some unpopular prerogatives.

Incorporation The process of creating 'corporate status', usually with a royal charter, by which an organisation, such as a trading company, acquires a legal status and powers analogous to those of an individual – e.g. ability to own property, or pursue legal proceedings, in its own name.

Jobbing   Used often in an unfavourable sense to describe dealing in, or manipulating, financial transactions for personal gain (as opposed to brokerage for a fixed fee).

Joint-stock   A collective investment by numerous individuals in a business enterprise carried on by a company organisation in their names.

Liquidity   The condition of having ready money or securities which can be quickly converted into cash.

Long-term borrowing   Loosely applied to borrowing which explicitly deferred repayment for many years, generally in excess of ten.

Mortgage   The conditional transfer of real property (i.e., land) by a borrower to his creditor, with the proviso that ownership and occupation remains with the borrower as long as he repays the loan, with due interest, by an agreed date.

Negotiable   Legal attribute of bills*, bonds*, promissory notes and other assignable* financial documents, which may be capable of being transferred (usually by endorsement*) to new rightful owners and thus capable of circulating like banknotes.

Option   An entitlement (to buy, or sell, a stock or share at a future date) acquired in return for a small fee.

Par   Abbreviation for parity, indicating an equality between the face-value and the current market value of a stock or share. Par can be indicated as 100 (per cent). 101 indicates a premium of 1%; 99 indicates a discount of 1%.

Premium   An increase or addition to the face value of a security; the opposite of a discount.

'Redeemable'   A government stock capable of being repaid within a limited period.

Redemption   Repayment (by the government) of a loan.

'Scrip'   Abbreviation for 'subscription'; a receipt indicating payment of a first instalment towards the purchase of a stock or share.

Scriveners   Lawyers, or notaries, specialising in drawing up legal documents such as conveyances of the ownership of land.

Securities   Loosely used to cover a wide range of title-deeds to ownership of a financial investment, such as stocks, shares, bonds, bills.

Share   Generally applied to the document (or 'security') recording an investment in a company, representing a share in its capital assets.

10 Price, Daniel, *Mechanisms of Evolution, 129* (London, 1717)

11 Foucault, M., *The Order of Things* (London, 1970)

12 Elton, G. R., *The Practice of History* (Oxford, 1967)

13 Hempel, C. (ed.), *The Philosophy of Natural Sciences* (Oxford, 1965)

14 Humboldt, A., *Essay on the Geography of Plants* (London, 1805)

15 Ibid.

16 Kuhn, T. S. (ed.), *The Structure of Scientific Revolutions* (Cambridge, 1962)

17 Lamb, H. H., *Climate, History and the Modern World* (London, 1982)

18 McCloskey, D., *The Rhetoric of Economics* (Madison, 1985)

19 Mill, J. S. (ed.), *A System of Logic* (London, 1886)

20 Mokyr, J., *The Lever of Riches* (Oxford, 1990)

21 Nelson, R. R., *The Sources of Economic Growth* (Cambridge, 1996)

22 Popper, K., *The Logic of Scientific Discovery* (London, 1959)

23 Rostow, W. W. (ed.), *The Stages of Economic Growth* (Cambridge, 1960)

24 Rosenberg, N. and Birdzell, L. E., *How the West Grew Rich* (Oxford, 1986)

SECONDARY SOURCES AND ARTICLES

25 Wallace, R., 'Population and Economic Problems' (1753), and
    'Various essays', *Essays XIV*, in *The Collected Works of R. Wallace, and the Naturalist*, pp. 50–95

26 Weber, M., *The Protestant Ethic* (New York, 1958)

27 White, K. D., 'The use of natural land problem in the past and the nineteenth century', *Economica* (London)

28 Wilson, J. B., 'The process of the economic', *(London)*

10 Defoe, Daniel, *The Anatomy of Exchange-Alley* (London, 1719).

11 Gardiner, S. R., *The Constitutional Documents of the Puritan Revolution, 1628–1660* (Oxford University Press, 1906).

12 Grey, A., *Debates in the House of Commons, 1667–94*, 10 vols (London, 1763).

13 Horwitz, H. (ed.), *The Parliamentary Diary of Narcissus Luttrell, 1691–93* (Oxford University Press, 1972).

14 Houghton, J., *A Collection for Improvement of Husbandry and Trade* (London, 1692–1703).

15 *Journals of the House of Commons*, vols 8–10 (London, 1742).

16 Kenyon, J. P. (ed.), *The Stuart Constitution, 1603–1688* (Cambridge University Press, 1966).

17 Letwin, W., *The Origins of Scientific Economics: English Economic Thought 1660–1776* (Methuen, 1963).

18 McCulloch, J. R. (ed.), *Early English Tracts on Commerce* (1856), (reprinted Cambridge University Press, 1954).

19 McCulloch, J. R. (ed.), *Old and Scarce Tracts on Money* (1856) (reprinted P. S. King & Son, 1933).

20 Mortimer, J., *Every Man his Own Broker* (London, 1801), republished in facsimile (Gregg International, 1969).

21 Postlethwayt, J., *The History of the Public Revenue* (London, 1759), republished in facsimile (Gregg International, 1971).

22 Prinsterer, G. van, *Archives ou correspondance inédite de la maison d'Orange Nassau*, 2nd series, 5 (Leyden and Utrecht, 1861).

23 Shaw, W. A. (ed.), *Select Tracts and Documents Illustrative of English Monetary History, 1626–1730* (1896) (republished G. Harding, 1935).

24 Thirsk, J. and Cooper, J. P. (eds), *17th Century Economic Documents* (Oxford University Press, 1972).

SECONDARY SOURCES; BOOKS AND ARTICLES

25 Aalbers, J., 'Holland's Financial Problems (1713–1733) and the Wars against Louis XIV', in Duke, A. C. and Tamse, C. A. (eds) *Britain and the Netherlands. Vol. 6. War and Society* (Martinus Nijhoff, 1977) pp. 79–93.

26 Acres, W., *The Bank of England from Within, 1694–1900*, 2 vols (Oxford University Press, 1931).

27 Allen, R. C., 'The price of freehold land and the interest rate in the seventeenth and the eighteenth centuries', *Economic History Review*, 2nd series, 41 (1988) pp. 33–50.

28 Alsop, J. D., 'The politics of Whig economics: the National

Debt on the eve of the South Sea Bubble', *Durham University Journal*, new series, 46 (1985) pp. 211–18.

29 Anderson, B. L., 'The attorney and the local capital market in Lancashire', in Harris, J. R. (ed.), *Liverpool and Merseyside: Essays in the Economic and Social History of the Port and its Hinterland* (Frank Cass, 1969).

30 Anderson, B. L., 'Provincial aspects of the Financial Revolution of the eighteenth century', *Business History*, 11 (1969) pp. 11–22.

31 Anderson, B. L., 'Money and the structure of credit in the eighteenth century', *Business History*, 12 (1970) pp. 85–101.

32 Appleby, J. O., *Economic Thought and Ideology in Seventeenth-Century England* (Princeton University Press, 1978).

33 Ashley, M., *Financial and Commercial Policy under the Cromwellian Protectorate* (Oxford University Press, 1935) (reprinted Cass, 1962).

34 Ashton, R., *The Crown and the Money Market 1603–1640* (Oxford University Press, 1960).

35 Ashton, T. S., *Economic Fluctuations in England 1700–1800* (Oxford University Press, 1959).

36 Aylmer, G., 'Place Bills and the Separation of Powers', *Transactions of the Royal Historical Society*, 5th series, 15 (1965) pp. 45–69.

37 Barbour, V., 'Marine risks and insurance in the seventeenth century', *Journal of Economic and Business History*, 1 (1928–29) pp. 561–96.

38 Barbour, V., *Capitalism in Amsterdam in the 17th Century* (Johns Hopkins Press, 1950).

39 Baxter, S. B., *The Development of the Treasury, 1660–1702* (Longman, 1957).

40 Beckett, J. V., 'Land tax or Excise: the levying of taxation in seventeenth- and eighteenth-century England', *English Historical Review*, 100 (1985) pp. 285–308.

41 Bisschop, W. R., *The Rise of the London Money Market 1640–1826* (P. S. King & Son, 1910).

42 Bowen, H.V., 'Investment and empire in the later eighteenth century: East India stockholding 1756–1791', *Economic History Review*, 2nd series, 42 (1989) pp. 186–206.

43 Brewer, J., *The Sinews of Power. War, Money and the English State 1688–1783* (Unwin & Hymans, 1989).

44 Brooks, C., 'Public Finance and Political Stability: the

78 Eagly, R. V. and Smith, V. K., 'Domestic and international integration of the London money market, 1731–1789', *Journal of Economic History*, Vol. 36 (1976) pp. 198–212.

79 Earle, P., 'Age and accumulation in the London business community, 1665–1720', in McKendrick, N. and Outhwaite, R. B. (eds), *Business Life and Public Policy: Essays in honour of D. C. Coleman* (Cambridge University Press, 1986).

80 Ewen, C. L'E., *Lotteries and Sweepstakes* (Heath Cranton, 1932).

81 Feavearyear, A. E., *The Pound Sterling. A History of English Money*, 2nd edition (Oxford University Press, 1963).

82 Floud, R. and McCloskey, D. (eds), *The Economic History of Britain since 1700*. Vol. 1 (Cambridge University Press, 1981).

83 Fores, M., 'The myth of a British Industrial Revolution', *History*, 66 (1981) pp. 181–90.

84 Grassby, R., 'The rate of profit in seventeenth-century England', *English Historical Review*, 84 (1969) pp. 721–51.

85 Grassby, R., 'English merchant capitalism in the seventeenth century. The composition of business fortunes', *Past & Present*, 46 (1970) pp. 87–107.

86 Grassby, R., 'The personal wealth of the business community in seventeenth-century England', *Economic History Review*, 2nd series, 23 (1970) pp. 220–34.

87 Habakkuk, H. J., 'Public finance and the sale of confiscated property during the Interregnum', *Economic History Review*, 2nd series, 15 (1962–63) pp. 70–88.

88 Harper, W. P., 'Public borrowing, 1640–1660'. Unpublished London University M.Sc. thesis (1929).

89 Hargreaves, E. L., *The National Debt* (Edward Arnold, 1930).

90 Harriss, G. L., 'Aids, loans and benevolences', *Historical Journal*, 6 (1963) pp. 1–19.

91 Hayton, D., 'The "Country" interest and the party system', in Jones, C. (ed.), *Party and Management in Parliament, 1660–1784* (University of Leicester Press, 1984).

92 Helleiner, K. F., *The Imperial Loans: A Study in Financial and Diplomatic History* (Oxford University Press, 1965).

93 Hewitt, V. H. and Keyworth, J. M., *As Good As Gold. 300 Years of British Bank Note Design* (The British Museum, 1987).

94 Hill, B. W., 'The change of government and the "loss of the City" 1710–1711', *Economic History Review*, 2nd series, 24 (1971) pp. 395–413.

95 Hirst, D., 'The conciliatoriness of the Cavalier Commons reconsidered', *Parliamentary History*, 6 (1987) pp. 221–35.

96 Holden, J. M., *The History of Negotiable Instruments in English Law* (University of London, Athlone Press, 1955).

97 Holderness, B. A., 'Widows in pre-industrial society: their economic functions', in Smith, R. M. (ed.), *Land, Kinship and Life-Cycle* (Cambridge University Press, 1985).

98 Holderness, B. A., 'Credit in English rural life before the nineteenth century, with special reference to the period 1650–1720', *Agricultural History Review*, 24 (1976) pp. 97–109.

99 Holderness, B. A., 'Credit in a rural economy, 1660–1800: some neglected aspects of probate inventories', *Midland History*, 3 (1975–76) pp. 94–116.

100 Holmes, G., 'The attack on "the influence of the Crown", 1702–1714', *Bulletin of the Institute of Historical Research*, 39 (1966) pp. 47–68.

101 Holmes, G., 'Gregory King and the Social Structure of Pre-Industrial England', *Transactions of the Royal Historical Society*, 5th series, 27 (1977) pp. 41–68.

102 Holmes, G., *British Politics in the Age of Anne*, revised edition (The Hambledon Press, 1987).

103 Holmes, G., *Augustan England: Professions, State and Society, 1680–1730* (Allen & Unwin, 1982).

104 Hoppit, J., 'The use and abuse of credit in eighteenth-century England', in McKendrick, N. and Outhwaite, R. B. (eds), *Business Life and Public Policy: Essays in honour of D. C. Coleman* (Cambridge University Press, 1986).

105 Hoppit, J., 'Financial crises in eighteenth-century England', *Economic History Review*, 2nd series, 39 (1986) pp. 39–58.

106 Hoppit, J., *Risk and Failure in English Business, 1700-1800* (Cambridge University Press, 1987).

107 Horsefield, J. K., 'The "Stop of the Exchequer" revisited', *Economic History Review*, 2nd series, 35 (1982) pp. 511–28.

108 Horsefield, J. K., *British Monetary Experiments, 1650–1710* (London School of Economics/G. Bell & Sons, 1960).

109 Horwitz, H., *Parliament, Policy and Politics in the Reign of William III* (Manchester University Press, 1977).

110 Horwitz, H., 'The East India trade, the politicians and the constitution, 1689–1702', *Journal of British Studies*, 17 (1978) pp. 1–18.

111 Hudson, P., 'The role of banks in the finance of the West

95. Pirci, D. "The coal reformers of the Carolina Commons," *Journal of Economic History*, vol. 6 (1967), pp. 721-38.

96. Holdness, M. *The Rings of Saturn: Narrative Formation in English*, Yale University of Princeton, Ashford Press, 1955.

97. Anderson, B. R. "Wages in pre-industrial society," in *Economic Structure*, ed. Roddis, R. M. (ed.). Bann, Knotty and Lee Col., Cambridge: Cambridge University Press, 1981.

98. Hodgcross, D. A. "Seville in England and the Peace in the eighteenth century, with special reference to Gui," *Journal of Social History*, vol. 6 (1972), pp. 95-106.

99. Hodgcross, B. A. "The Tangle in a rural economy, 1660-1800: some analytical aspects of a pattern," *Social History*, vol. 54 (1975-76), pp. 85-116.

100. Elston, G. R. "The effect on the inflation of the Crown," *Past & Present: Bulletin of the Society of Historical Research*, vol. 46 (1963), pp. 11-14.

101. Thirsk, J. "Inequalities in land tenure in the Social Revolution of England," *Transactions of the Royal Historical Society*, 5th series, 24 (1974), pp. 41-53.

102. Thirsk, J. *Economic Policy and the Use of Later-seventeenth-century England*, London: Jackson Press, 1967.

103. Thirsk, J. *Economy and Society, the English Poor and Social Change*, Leicester: Leicester School, 1987.

104. Hoppen, H. "The use and abuse of credit, the eighteenth-century England," in *McKendrick, N. S.* and University, P. B. (eds.), *Culture and Politics in the Eighteenth Century, Honour of J. D. C.*, Cambridge: Cambridge University Press, 1976.

105. Hopkins, S. *The rural crisis of the eighteenth-century England*, London: Ashgate Press, vol. 6 (1966), pp. 52-51.

106. Hoplin, K. *Price and Society: English Institutions, 1660-1850*, Cambridge: Cambridge University Press, 1965.

107. Hawkeday, J. S. "The Story of the beginning," in *Economic History Review*, 2nd series, 33 (1979), pp. 31-8.

108. Householder, R. C. *Banking and Society in Germany, 1830-1870*, London: School of Economics, Hull & Sons, 1968.

109. Howell, H. "Money, Inheritance and Estate," in *Rowe of William D. Middleton*, Bloomington: Indiana University Press, 1970.

110. Howlett, H. "The Case Study of the Inflation and the distribution, 1660-1700," *Journal of Historical Studies*, 1 (1958), pp. 1-16.

111. Hudson, P. "The role of funds in the future of the West..."

145 Murphy, A. E., *Richard Cantillon: Entrepreneur and Economist* (Oxford University Press, 1986).

146 Neal, L. D., 'Interpreting power and profit in economic history: a case study of the Seven Years War', *Journal of Economic History*, 37 (1977) pp. 31–5.

147 Neal, L., 'The integration of international capital markets. Quantitative evidence from the eighteenth to the twentieth centuries', *Journal of Economic History*, 45 (1985) pp. 219–26.

148 Newman, K., *Financial Marketing and Communications* (Holt, Rinehart & Winston, 1984).

149 Nichols, G. O., 'Intermediaries and the development of English government borrowing: the case of Sir John James and Major Robert Huntingdon, 1675–79', *Business History*, 29 (1987) pp. 27–46.

150 Nichols, G. O., 'English Government Borrowing, 1660–1688', *Journal of British Studies*, 10 (1971) pp. 83–104.

151 Nichols, G. O., 'The development of English repayment and interest rates: an examination of government borrowing and the loans of Sir Stephen Fox, 1667–1674', *Revue Internationale d'Histoire de la Banque*, 30–31 (1985) pp. 247–65.

152 O'Brien, P. K., 'The political economy of British taxation, 1660–1815', *Economic History Review*, 2nd series, 41 (1988) pp. 1–32.

153 Outhwaite, R. B., 'The trials of foreign borrowing: the English crown and the Antwerp money market in the mid-sixteenth century', *Economic History Review*, 2nd series, 19 (1966) pp. 289–305.

154 Plumb, J. H., *Sir Robert Walpole*, 2 vols (Cresset Press, 1957, 1960).

155 Plumb, J. H., *The Growth of Political Stability in England, 1675–1725* (Macmillan, 1967).

156 Powell, E. T., *The Evolution of the Money Market* (The Financial News, 1915).

157 Pressnell, L. S., *Country Banking in the Industrial Revolution* (Oxford University Press, 1956).

158 Pressnell, L. S., 'Public monies and the development of English banking', *Economic History Review*, 2nd series, 5 (1952–53) pp. 378–97.

159 Price, J. M., *Capital and Credit in British Overseas Trade. The View from the Chesapeake, 1700–1776* (Harvard University Press, 1980).

160 Price, J. M., 'Notes on some London Price-Currents, 1667–

1715', *Economic History Review*, 2nd series, 7 (1954–55) pp. 240–50.

161 Price, J. M., 'The excise crisis of 1733', in Baxter, S. B. (ed.), *England's Rise to Greatness, 1688–1763* (University of California Press, 1983).

162 Reitan, E. A., 'The civil list in eighteenth-century British politics: parliamentary supremacy versus the independence of the crown', *Historical Journal*, 9 (1966) pp. 318–37.

163 Reitan, E. A. , 'From Revenue to Civil List, 1688–1702: The Revolution Settlement and the "Mixed and Balanced" Constitution', *Historical Journal*, 13 (1970) pp. 571–88.

164 Richards, R. D., 'A pre-Bank of England banker – Edward Backwell', *Economic History*, 1 (1929) pp. 335–55.

165 Richards, R. D., *The Early History of Banking in England* (P. S. King & Son, 1929).

166 Riley, J. C., *International Government Finance and the Amsterdam Capital Market, 1740–1815* (Cambridge University Press, 1980).

167 Riley, J. C., *The Seven Years War and the Old Regime in France* (Princeton University Press, 1986).

168 Roberts, C., 'The constitutional significance of the financial settlement of 1690', *Historical Journal*, 20 (1977) pp. 59–76.

169 Rogers, N., 'Money, land and lineage; the big bourgeoisie of Hanoverian London', *Social History*, 4 (1979) pp. 437–54.

170 Rogers, P., *Eighteenth Century Encounters. Studies in Literature and Society in the Age of Walpole* (Harvester Press, 1985).

171 Roseveare, H. G., 'The Advancement of the King's Credit, 1660–1672', unpublished Cambridge University Ph.D. thesis (1962).

172 Roseveare, H. G., [Review of Dickson, P. G. M. (**72**)] *Economic Journal*, 78 (1968) pp. 458–61.

173 Roseveare, H. G., *The Treasury. The Evolution of a British Institution* (Allen Lane, 1969).

174 Roseveare, H. G., *The Treasury 1660–1870. The Foundations of Control* (Allen & Unwin, 1973).

175 Roseveare, H. G., 'Government borrowing and the rate of interest in the late seventeenth century', in *Prodotto lordo e finanza pubblica* [Proceedings of the Istituto Internazionale di Storia Economica 'Francesco Datini', Prato, 1976].

176 Roseveare, H. G., 'Finances', in Latham, R. (ed.), *The Diary of Samuel Pepys*, Vol. 10, *Companion* (Bell & Hyman, 1983) pp. 130–7.

177 Roseveare, H. G., 'Prejudice and policy: Sir George Downing

Bibliography

159. Chinnery Martin *Penrup*. 2nd series 7 (1923–25), pp. 236–40.

161. Price L M., The erotic tradition 1882, in Bayley S. R. (ed.) *Fashion, Arts in Graphics*, pp. 273–283, University of California Press (1982).

162. Priori R. L., 'Civilised in multiform century British politics and mannering supervisory servis ... its understanding philosophy', *Modern Archeology* 9 (1906), pp. 118–42.

163. Relph E. A., 'Form Roman. Roman Civil Dist 1688–1702 The Revolution Settlement and the Mixed and Balanced Constitution', *Historian Journal* 6 (1979), pp. 471–88.

164. Richards S. D., 'Anglo-Liberal England Oxford Oxford Richmell *Economy Journal* (1929) pp. 53–78.

165. Reynolds R. D. *The Sun. Principles of Revenue in Bargans*, V & K Siou, Sons, 1934.

166. Rley L. C., *International margin. Theory and the Industrial Capital Issues 1940–1972*, Cambridge University Press (1980).

167. Rriley J. C. *Dutch side Roon. Financ and the Age Paris in France* (Princeton University Press 1986).

168. Roberson C. 'The constitutional significance of the financial requirements 1688, *Historical Journal* 20 (1977), pp. 59–76.

169. Rboley. N. 'Money, land and the ... double banking role of the British London *Social History* 1 (1978), pp. 117–57.

170. Rogers R., *Research Century Commerce Banking ... in Spring and the reign of the Earl about, Manchester Press 1985.

171. Rosevear H. D., 'The Treasury and the King's Credit 1660–1672', (unpublished Cambridge University Ph.D thesis 1962).

172. Rosevear H. G., 'The Inventor the Thesis C. R. M. (721) ... in *Journal* 26 (1983) pp. 136–48.

173. Rabertson R. B., *The Treasury: The Evolution of a Public Department* (Allen Lane 1969).

174. Savanner H. L., W., *Treasure Done the Arts. Pushers of Combat* (Allen & Unwin 1935).

175. Scoville H. G., 'Government borrowing and the Financing and in the late seventeenth century', in *Finances française deux ordres: Distribution of the Interior financière de Sault Perpignan Florence French Public Wars 1986*.

176. Schumpeter H. G., 'Finances', in Lehman Rickel J., *The Penn D. Smithee Press Vol 10. Cambridge, Oed & Olympia 1960*, pp. 376–9.

177. Skenner H. B., *The prosperous politics. Soul Own Reformation Ist 1971*.

Index